Soulja's Story

Mr. A.I.T.

ISBN: 978-1-4269-5728-4 (sc)
ISBN: 978-1-4269-5953-0 (e)

Trafford rev. 06/02/2011

 www.trafford.com

North America & international
toll-free: 1 888 232 4444 (USA & Canada)
phone: 250 383 6864 ✦ fax: 812 355 4082

From the author-

I dedicate this book to all my brothers and sisters in the Indiana Department of Correction- for I am you. I want you brothers and sisters to stay strong, and remember hope is alive and dreams do come true. I would also like to dedicate this book to Madear my grandma, who, by the grace of God, has never left my side while I was being abandoned by so many friends who claimed they loved me and had my back. And my beautiful children who never stopped loving me even when I wasn't or couldn't be there. Last but not least, I'd like to dedicate this book to the very few friends who did stick with me and never stopped believing in me.

- May God bless you all, as he has blessed me.

Soulja's Story

"Everybody gets down!" yelled Soulja when he entered First National Bank. Then ten tofifteen customers fell faster than dominoes noticing the tall masked man dressed in black, waving a sub machine gun and ready to blast the first motherfucker who didn't want to comply. The security guard thought Soulja was slippin, because his back was turned to him. Catching a bank robber would get him publicity on a whole different level, he thought. He drew his thirty eight from his holster, but he couldn't take aim, an old woman with fussy hair wearing a flower-printed dress had already peeped his play. She was close to the guard, lying on the floor with the other customers. But, she wasn't a customer at all. T was Soulja's best friend and number one soldier, her name was Special. Special pulled the baby nine millimeter with the built in laser beam out her purse and without thinking put a slug though the side of the guards head. Watching as he fell to the ground beside her. The female smiled at her handiwork because she knew he would've tried to kill Soulja. She upheld her vow to eradicate anyone trying to do him. Soulja never even glanced back since he knew Special had everything under control behind him. Soulja hit the tellers quickly because the safe would take too long, and time was everything in the bank robberies. Everything was going as planned, they were barely at one minute when Special saw the FEDs jacking their gateway driver and surrounding the exits. She told Soulja, who immediately wondered did he move too slowly this time, giving a clerk enough time to signal

1

the silent alarm. He brushed off the thought, knowing he didn't. Then the thought hit him as he put the last cash into the duffle e bag- *someone had snitched, but who?* He vowed to find out and make sure they paid with their life, but first he had to get them out of this bank because they refused to go to prison. And they meant it....

<u>The Set Up</u>

"What up Soulja?"

"It's all good Christine; what's up with you?"

"Motherfucker, my name Special, don't get it twisted!"

"Girl, fuck you. I know what the fuck yo name is. I gave it to you, didn't I?"

"Yeah, that's why I didn't blast yo yellow ass for using my government name." – She returned.

"Girl please- you already know if you pull ya chopper on me, Ill bury it wit you. So quit rapping and get yo fat ass up and blaze the weed."

"Whatever nigga, you know aint shit fat on me but ass, thighs, and pockets." (She wasn't lying either because this sister's five six or seven frame was stacked. She carried one forty five around very well with her dark brown skin and shoulder-length hair when she didn't cut it.

Special had nice, firm breast and an ass that threatened to bust out of everything she put on.

She wasn't one of the dime-pieces Soulja messed around with, but she had heart and loyalty that put her in a class by herself. Plus, she was a boss freak. Always wanting to be Soulja's girl, even before she met him, Special would hear about how real he was and that he didn't take shit form anybody. Not to mention he was about getting money.

One of her sisters were dating Soulja's partner Demond. Special found out he was about to be released from prison after doing five years of a ten

3

year plea bargain for shooting a local drug dealer over a bogus deal. The dealer was supposed to sell Soulja half a key of coke for the nine grand, but, at the meeting he tried to go up on the price. And the quality wasn't even pure as the sample he gave Soulja a few days in advance.

An argument ensued that ended with the shyster being shot three times in his chest. But, fate would spare his life and fear would make him tell the cops who done it, and agree to testify in court. He lied about the reason for the shooting, which the police could tell, but they didn't give a shit. They finally had a case that would stick on Soulja in prison Soulja, or Ronnie Parelli, read street books, got his GED, and hustled a little, but most of his time was spent plotting his release and hitting the weight pile. He left the joint twenty nine years old; a hundred and ninety pound of solid muscle looking good on his six-frame. Soulja kept his head shaved bald, plus he acquired lots of tattoos while incarcerated and you could see them well on this light skinned man on a mission.

About a week after his release, Soulja was chilling with Mesha, his ex, plus Crystal and Marie, his daughters. He couldn't believe how big his girls had gotten over the few years apart from them. Mesha always brought them to visit while he was down, but still he really just notice.

He has been there for two and a half hours when his boy Demond came by to pick him up.

He told his daughter he'd see them the following day, kissed them and then left. But not before checking out baby momma with them little shorts. Half her ass protruded from the bottom of those shorts, and she knew he'd like it since she'd gotten thicker since he left. He and Mesha still cared about each other and would occasionally sleep together when either or both were horny.

Soulja expected Demond to be alone but there was a girl in the car with him. He'd never seen her before so he said what's up and jumped in the back seat of Deamonds' '95 Coupe Deville with chrome twenties sounds and wet paint. At first sight you'd think the brother was a dealer, but he was just a dam good mechanic with dope-boy tendencies. They used to hustle together before Soulja got popped off. After that Demond got a job and kept it although he might occasionally sell a couple week sacks here and there; nothing really to get in trouble about though.

Soulja thought the chick in front was one of Demond's girls because the nigga kept a flock of them at all times. So, he told Demond to drop him off at the crib. His guy then asked the chick, whose name was Christine, where was she going, and out of the blue she stated she was going home with Soulja, and then asked if she could go with him.

She questioned caught him off guard, but she was desirable. ~ She girl told him about what she'd heard in the streets and how she couldn't wait to meet him personally. She was a stone-cold freak, too. She sucked his dick for what seemed like an eternity, and then rode him for a while until he was ready to turn her over into the doggy-style position which was Soulja's favorite especially when a girl had a fat ass like Christine's and could take some dick. She would end up pleasing him for about a week straight in that manner.

They became acquainted during that time and he realized just how street she was. She'd sold rocks out the local projects, carried a small .25 automatic on her person, and he actually believed she'd use it in a heartbeat. Soulja liker her- but she was falling in love with him fast. He spruced her up with game and the rest was history.

Soulja was relaxing on the couch watching her walk back and forth talking to him with a blunt in her mouth, while dressed in booty shorts and a sports bra. He loved the way her ass shook whenever she walked. It really made him horny, but at the moment they had business to tend to. Therefore, he brushed the thought off and cleared his mind's slate.

"Pass the weed and go get dressed. We gotta roll; its getting late and Milky said the nigga would be at Shaw's by midnight."

"Alright Baby, here. Don't forget the plan cause this supposed to be a sweet lick. Plus, I've seen this cake ass nigga stuntin in that white Caddy truck on twenty foes, rolling down Broadway one day." Milky was a stripper from Shangrala. Five-five and a dark-skinned brick –house that did the booty shake better than tip drill. Soulja had been sleeping with her for a while and she let him know about any marks that came around. He'd been having Milky drawn close to a baller named slick ever since he showed up in the club flossing platinum links. Telling her all about the money he was getting in Gary and Chicago.

She knew most of the niggas that came through those doors had some type of story so they could get some pussy, but most of the time they were frontin and she knew it. However, after researching Slick she knew he was the Truth is nigga had major cake, a tight crew of wannabe killers, houses all over the place, a clothing store on the Westside of Chicago, and he rode with no less than ten stacks on him at all times and probably close to fifty in jewelry.

His shit was tight all the way around the table. Except for one thing, this nigga talked way too much after a couple of good fucks from Milky. He really thought she was down with him, but as saying goes, you can't trust a big butt and a smile. She juiced the nigga for several months, getting as much information as she could. So tonight was the night.

She told Slick about her girl Tina a.k.a Special, and how thick, cute, and plus how much of a freak she was. Milky was to meet him at Shaws by 12:30. The plan was to separate the mark from his security -two young weed heads out to prove themselves.

Dre and Brandon was a couple of rough necks from the eastside of Gary that stayed in trouble. Slick put them on his team after he watched them beat a nigga half to death over a dime bag of weed .As security, they stayed close to Slick wherever he went and tonight was no different.

Slick stepped in the club sporting an all white Versace hookup with the black and white gators. He had bling on everywhere it would fit; neck, wrist, ears, and fingers. Milky admitted to herself that nigga did look good, but to bad cause he's the mark. She didn't look to bad herself in a skin –tight, all black cat suit that showed off her curves perfectly.

Stiletto pumps and her red bra and thong set influenced her to play the part to a tee. They set in a booth and ordered something to drink while waiting on Special-well she was Tina tonight.

Wearing her short, fuck me skirt minus the bra and panties, Special strutted in around 12:15 with her top exposing her stomach and belly piercing. She looked good tonight and Slick thought so too. He couldn't wait to get these chicks in the bed naked .She walked up to their booth and sat down. What's up' Tee?' said Milky. "Slick, Tee, and Tee Slick." She introduced them. What's up Tee?" "What you drinking tonight?" asked Slick. "Hennessey and coke."

Tina replied, smiling. Slick ordered doubles for everybody.

Shaws was wall-to-wall packed. You had to rub bodies just to make your way through the crowd, and the music banged where you had to yell in order to be heard. This is what all the many club hoppers hope for.

"Let's dance," Milky offered her girl, Tina.

I'll watch yall do yall thang," said Slick.

Girl, let's give this nigga a show," Milky told Tina while they were out of hearing distance.

"Fasho girl."

They showed out, too. I mean they grinded on each other, tongue kissed, and shook their asses to the likes of , 'In Da Club, by Fifty Cent, 'Draped Up' by Bun B, and some Lil John and the eastside boys. Slick watched with his buzz on and was just about ready to roll out .

Across the street from the club a 1987 Chevy –black with limo tent–was parked. Inside Soulja, Lou, and Big Tye plotted and went over the plan.

"Those niggas right there, "Soulja pointed.

"Which ones?', asked Lou." The black three hunnit, or the white caddy truck?'

Damn, both of 'em dubbed and chromed out." Big Tye added. "Yeah, if they live through the night." Lou joked.

"Well that's on them, but follow the plan."

The trio were strapped up packing top 05Rugers with extended clips while Lou had a .357 Dessert Eagle with the laser beam. Big Tye felt more enthused by his chrome fifty cal.

They all met in the joint a few years prior. Soulja liked them and realized they were some real brothas. They kicked it around the yard in prison and he told them to get at him when they get out. And that's what they did. Soulja felt close to them because all their stories were alike–all grew up in the ghetto in single parent homes, hit the streets young where they stole, robbed, hustled and killed whenever they had to. To get what they wanted. Still, Soulja was older, so they looked u to him. Plus, they knew he was crazy ass hell.

"Hey, ain't somebody in that three hunnit?' Lou asked.

"Yeah." Soulja answered." His lil security, so they must be about to roll. So get ready." He prompted the crew. Being that it was like four in the morning, Slick told the girls to get ready to roll. They were buzzing real good when they exited the club and headed towards the truck. Special glazed out the side of her eyes, noticing the Chevy sitting where it should have been. She smiled to herself because she knew this was a lame as nigga. Slick was paying any attention to nothing but her and Milky's asses as they threw them out of proportion while walking to the truck.

She was right; that's just what he was doing too. Taking up the rear and starting at her sensual curves while floating to the ride. Slick went over to the 300 while letting the ladies in the truck.

"Wake the fuck up, nigga!' He banged on the passenger's window at Dre. Both occupants in the car jumped startled." You niggas smoke to much weed; sitting up here sleep when yall suppose to be on point." "We up man. Let's go get something to eat. We hungry as hell."

Brandon replied. What's up with them hoes, Slick? Put us on?' Dre asked.

"Not tonight, lil nigga. I'm on something, but I got yall next time. Follow me to the gas station so ole girl can get some squares. Plus, I need to get some condoms anyway, then we can get some grub." 'Cool , "Brandon, the driver of the 300 agreed." And stay the fuck woke niggas. This is my time; sleep on y'all time." Aite man Dre answered.But in his head he was saying fuck you nigga, I'm tired and high. Slick walked back and got behind the wheel of the already running vehicle. The girls were inside watching 'Belly on the drop screen when he entered. Looking like they were ready for whatever. "Yall ready to do this shit, or what?' He double checked with the two females for reassurance. 'Nawl, nigga. Are you ready to do us?' Tina leaned over to the front seat squeezing on Milky's tits. Slick just smiled and pulled off, feeling excited. With in the 300 in tow and the dark Chevy a half block behind, lurking. They might have noticed death following them in their rear view mirror, if those two niggas weren't so fucked up off that weed and drank, but they were slippin. They both were strapped with glocks, but Dre's heat didn't have one in the chamber and Brandon's was up under the seat.

Slick drove into the lot of a dull-lit 24 hr gas station right off the highway. He was too busy thinking about pussy to wonder why Special told him to go there. The gas station held one attendant who happens to be Soulja's guy, Terrence, from the block. e only reason Terrence had the job was because he was on parole after being released from prison six months prior on drug charges. His uncle owned the gas station; that's how he ended up there, but he was still in the game. Still down for the set, and knew exactly what was about to go down, Slick pulled the Caddy truck up to the side of the gas station.

Milky had Slick to pull over there because it had a restroom. There was a big , blue garbage can next to where he parked. Slick didn't like the set up, but brushed it off since he had two of his boy with him. e 300 pulled in a few spaces away and Brandon got out in order to holler at Slick. Dre had dozed back off with his pistol in his lap.

"I'm bout to use the restroom." Milky climbed out of the truck.

"Aite, shorty. I'll tell Brandon to get the squares for ya girl." Sending half of his security in for cigarettes and condoms while he and Tina sat and chilled. The Chevy drove into the lot like a minute later and the driver pulled right up to a gas pump. Slick gazed at the car but only noticed one occupant, so he turned his attention back to Tina who was teasing and making him horny. She leaned back and opened her legs across the seat, revealing a bald, fat mound of monkey with no under wear covering it.

Can you handle all this?' Penetrating her pussy with her finger and tasting her own juices.

Slick thought about tasting it for himself right on the spot as two hood figures crept up from behind the building, slowly moving towards the truck. Before Slick could turn around, the door that Milky left unlocked was being opened by Soulja, who greeted him by slapping him in the face with a Ruger. Big Tye crept up on Dre while he was still asleep in the 300 with his gun in his lap. Tye woke Dre up, pushing the Dessert Eagle into his temple. Dre looked up and tried to reach for the burner, but Tye already had it.

"You looking for this?" Showing dude his own gun. "What you want, nigga?" Dre asked, getting real scared. 'Your life if you don't shut the fuck up, nigga."

Inside the station Brandon noticed shit was messed up outside, but he left his gun in the ride.

He pulled his cell phone out to call for assistance, so Terrence pulled out a gage from behind the counter and made him hang it up.

All three men were tied up. Dre and Brandon were tossed in the trunk of the Chevy and Slick was thrown in the back of the Caddy truck, blindfolded.

Soulja took 9, 000 Slick had in his pocket and gave it to Terrence. Soulja, the girls, and Slick rode in the Caddy truck while Lou and Tye trailed in the Chevy and the 300.Slick kept trying to plead with Soulja from behind the blindfold, but was ignored because Soulja had already had everything planned out. Conversation was not apart of his plan. The whole kidnapping took less than three minutes, which pleased Soulja because he hated fuck-ups.

{Bring on the pain...}

They dropped Milky off and told her to call them in the morning. Soulja would take care of her. And she knew his word was good, so she said okay. Lou and Tye ditched the 300 and took Brandon and Dre to an old house that Soulja picked out which was in the boondocks, away from nosey neighbors. Soulja pulled in through the back yard off the alley and drug Slick in. He then led the man down into the basement.

The kidnapper took Slicks eyewear off and let Slick see his two boys tied up next to each other. Soulja sat Slick down in a third chair then tied him up also. Special walked into the room.

Ya'll bitches set me up!' Slick exclaimed." You set yo self up, nigga. Thinkin you couldn't be touched." Soulja replied after slapping the baller across the mouth with his gun."

And watch yo mouth, pussy." Disrespecting Slick real bad." Now where's the shit at?'

'What shit?' Soulja hit him again." The dope and money mothafucka!' splitting Slick's lip open." I don't sell dope no more man. I'm a business man. All my money in the bank. Y'all got my loot off me, man." You think we fuckin with yo punk ass!? Lou shoot that nigga.

Soulja pointed at Brandon, but , before Brandon could beg for his life Lou shot him twice through the chest, killing him instantly, blowing him and the chair backwards.

"Tell them what they wanna know man, I'm not trying to die." Dre demanded frantically.

His eyes watering.

'Shut yo punk ass up!" Slick said while bleeding from the mouth." Alright, man, but how I know y'all not gone kill us anyway after y'all get the shit?'

For one thing , nigga, I'm not scared of you or yo weak ass crew, and I'm bout my word. So if you cooperate right now I won't kill you."

Soulja already knew where a couple of Slick's pads were from the recon that Milky was doing, but each spot had nice security, So he needed pass codes for his security systems and where the dope and safe were, and which houses held what.

"Alright man, I got like fifty g's and a bird in a safe at this bitch crib on thirty fifth and Fillmore.' Slick said.

" I know that ain't it, nigga . You think I'm fuckin' stupid , don't you?" Soulja asked, feeling off ended.

"Naw man, it ain't like that." Slick answered, appearing to be sincere. 'One more time, nigga. Where it at?'

'I just told you man. What you want from me?'

Soulja knew he had to get the stubborn nigga's undivided attention, so he said one thing "Special." And just like that she came around and shot Slick in his left kneecap, making him scream out and cry from the pain. But, nobody could hear him in the muzzled, brick basement away from any neighbors.

"T at shit hurts, don't it? Now you done fucked up that nice outfit." Soulja reasoned with his agonizing victim. 'So you ready to talk to me, Playboy?'

'Okay-Okay!' Cried Slick in so much pain that he kept stuttering his words whenever he tried to talk.

"And no more bullshit." Soulja gave Special a pen and pad to write down the security pass codes, exactly where the safe was, and the address Soulja already knew about.

"Alright man. Let us go; you got what you need." Slick cried out, "Man, I need to go to the hospital!"

Dre was dead quiet, just literally praying to make it out alive. T is was the first time the really wanted out the game and to have a normal life. So, he vowed to himself that if he made it out alive, he was through. This situation scared him to death. Especially after what they did to his boy Brandon. He felt Slick treated them like shit, so he kinda enjoyed watching his cheap ass being tortured. But, still he was terrified. "Yo punk ass okay for now. Cause you ain't going no where before I make sure shit is where it's suppose to be, "said Soulja." Find something to wrap that nigga's legs up. Maybe he'll shut the fuck up." He continued while he and special were walking out the door. [**BINGO**]

They went to the address on the paper that Sick gave them. It was a two story brick house in a very nice neighborhood in Merriville. No one was suppose to be there, but Soulja checked his heat and told Special to do the same. He then looked at his watch and saw that daylight was soon approaching.

'Come on, let's do this before the street light's up and the neighbors notice I'm not Slick and call the cops.'

"Oh-that's why you drove his truck out here to throw off any nosy ass people." Special noted.

Exactly, but it's over if we don't hurry up." Soulja slowly opened the front door of the crib with his gun in his free hand and they walked in." So far , so good. Hit that code before the alarm goes off."

Special defused the alarm and they walked through the plushed out crib, noticing big screen tv's, fur rugs, Jacuzzis up and down stairs, with marbles floors.

"Damn, this bitch is plushed out, "said Special.

"T e safe is suppose to be in the master bedroom, in the closet."

When he turned on the light for the closet he seen the safe in the corner .He noticed how big it was, and knew he couldn't have gotten it out the house. So he was glad he had the combination." Let's see if this is right, seventeen left, twelve right." Click.

When the safe opened he smiled at Special who smiled back at him because inside they found over $200, 000 and at least 50 keys of uncut dope. Special found a couple of gym bags and loaded up the dope and money.

Let's go. We probably got like a half hour before the sun comes up, and we still gotta switch cars." Soulja commanded. He made sure to wipe anything they touched off before they left, and besides closing the safe back, he even reset the alarm.

'What about them niggas?' Special asked as they were riding away.

'Oh-yeah, call Lou's phone for me and tell him to put the phone on speaker." His assistant did so.

Lou turned on the speaker so everyone could here Soulja talking." Hey Slick."

"Yeah, Still in pain, ha moaned.

"Shit was where you said it would be."

"Well let us go , man." You got what you wanted , Slick replied.

"I told yo punk ass I was a man of my word, didn't I, nigga? I said I wouldn't kill you if shit was right , and shit is right, so they bout to free yall right now."

Soulja finished saying what he had to say and that was the last thing Slick heard before Lou put a bullet in his head with the Dessert Eagle. He tore off half of Slick's head with a slug from his gun and it didn't bother him at all.

"Man, please don't kill, "was all Dre got to say before Big Tye shot him through his heart and head.

The first shot killed him, but Tye didn't take chances anymore because he heard of niggas playing possum before.

"We gotta burn the crib and meet Soulja in the morning, Lou said. "Yeah, we gotta dump these heats. Tye agreed.

They torched the house with Slick, Dre and Brandon's bodies inside , threw the guns in the lake and made sure everything was tight, traded cars , then went to get something to eat at the truck stop before going to get some rest. They had to meet Soulja in the morning.

"Let's go get some sleep cause we got a big day ahead of us tomorrow ."Soulja said." First we gone fuck .~ en we gone sleep." Special returned. Soulja laughed, but he was down with it.

[Putting it down]

The next morning all the tops in Soulja's crew had text messages for them to meet at Sam's around noon. Sam's was a club on Fifth Ave. in Gary that Soulja had planned on buying from this Mexican guy once he looted up and had the right name to put on the paper work, because legally he was unemployed. He needed five hundred thousand for the club, liquor license, and a lot across from the club. e spot wasn't that big, but Soulja had plans for it so he had to get his money tight soon.

"Hello, Ronnie, are you up yet?"

"Yeah, what's up Mesha?" Mesha was Soulja's baby mom's and one of the few he didn't mind using his government name.

"I need you to come through here when you get out, okay?' "Is something wrong?"

"Naw boy, I just want to see you. Okay?'

"Alright , bye." Soulja knew if something was wrong she was about to ask him for some money. He still loved her, but he didn't want to be with her right now anyway because they stayed into it and he needed to be focused on business. So he stayed in her and the kids lives, and looked out when she needed him to.

"Who was that ?"Yo baby mizzle, "said Special. Dressed in a t-shirt and little black shorts.

"Yeah I gotta roll through there when I leave here." "I thought you had to meet the fellas at twelve?"

"It's only ten, girl I'll be there at twelve. You just roll down there and let them nigga's know I'll be there."

"Alright boss."

"You damn right , don' be questioning me ass hole."

"Whatever nigga, "They both laughed. Special was so much in love with him that she got jealous about Mesha, Knowing that Soulja still loved her even though they weren't together. She knew they were still sleeping with each other, but she wouldn't dare say anything about it.

Soulja and Special shared a plushed-out three bedroom with a full basement and two car garage. They weren't a couple even though she wanted to be one so bad. They had their own bedrooms, but that never stopped them from waking up after a night of weed, Hennessy, and a bunch of other shit. She would be Soulja's woman was all she kept saying to herself daily.

After taking a shower Soulja threw on his all-white Nike jogging suit, with the all white Nike dope man shoes, and white socks. He then grabbed his chrome-plated Ruger off the dresser then took a thousand dollars, and put it in his pocket, heading for the door.

After getting herself cleaned up, Special threw on a tight blue-jean outfit that showed her body shape very well with black walking shoes, a black hat and handbag that she kept her baby nine millimeter in.

"What time is it?" Soulja asked, noticing he left his Rolex in the bedroom.

"It's going on eleven." Following him out the door with a black gym bag in her hand. It was around seventy-five degrees outside with the sun shining bright, so it was nice for eleven a.m.

"Take the bag with you to the club and I'll meet you down there, okay!" Said Soulja.

"Alright."

"And be careful, too." Soulja cautioned.

"Don't worry about me; you just be careful." Special told him. they went to their separate cars and pulled off down the street.

Soulja jumped in his 94, Q45 Infinity, burgundy in color, leather seats wood grain, sunroof, with the dark limo tinted windows and factory five star rims. He kept his Q with the factory look to avoid attention with the cops, but he souped his engine up with a nitro kit just in case.

Special jumped in her all black cutlass with the leather seat's and nice, Boss sound system and twenty-inch five star rims. She threw the gym bag in her special-built stash spot in the trunk. She had her license and a gun permit. Soulja made sure she got them, especially the gun permit cause he couldn't get one being a felon.

Soulja moved Mesha and his kids into a nice, four bedroom crib in the Westside parts of the Glen park area in Gary right after he got back on his feet. He made sure they didn't want for anything, but Mesha was unappeasable.

[PO-PO's]

"What we got, Frank?"

"It looks like a homicide. The fire department got a call around six this morning about a house fire, but once they got the flames under control, they started finding bodies and realized it was arson to cover the murders."

Do we know who the victims are yet?" Asked Detective Jones." The bodies were burned real bad, so we won't know anything until the autopsies are complete, "answered Detective Wilson." This was a pretty good location for a crime considering the location not having neighbors, But maybe someone down the way saw something or someone leaving the area around the time of the fire that didn't belong around here. So have patrol to canvas the area and see what they turn up with."

Okay Frank. I'm on it."

Frank Wilson and Mark Jones were two roughneck detectives of the Gary Police Department. They both got their ass kicked in school, so now they got theirs on the streets by giving everyone a hard time, but they do get the job done with the most arrest in the precinct-especially in homicides.

"The captain is gonna want quick resolution with this case cause the mayor has been crawling up his ass about Gary being the murder capital again." Frank said.

Yeah, I know. So I'm gonna put some pressure on a few people, but first we need to find out who these guys are, cause all the other evidence was burned up in the fire."

{Baby Momma}

"What's up, Mesha." said Soulja walking in the house." Come in and sit down, nigga .You in a hurry or something?" Following her into the living room, noticing she wasn't wearing panties under the jogging pants she had on because her ass was jiggling, and she knew he was watching too.

"What time is it, cause I got to meet somebody at twelve?"

"Its fifteen after eleven., you got time." "Where are the girls?" He asked seeing that the house was too quiet.

"They're at my mom's." Mesha answered, smiling.

"Girl, what yo freak-ass smiling at? I got business to take care of." That's at twelve. Shit, I'm not asking you to make love to me nigga. I just want some dick from you."

Soulja tried to play the role like he didn't want sex from her, but he couldn't deny how good she was looking and all the weight she'd put on while he was locked up. Mesha stood like five-six or seven and only weighed maybe a hundred thirty pounds when he left, but now she had to be almost 160, and the only fat was ass, big thighs, and tits to come with it.

"I'll come back later tonight after I take care of my business, "said Soulja, standing up.

Quit playing boy, "walking up to him, sticking her hand down the front of his joggers, grabbing his dick and kissing on his neck, at the same time making him instantly erect. They had history together, so she knew how to get him where she wanted him, and he knew it too.

They started kissing briefly. Then, Soulja turned Mesha around and bent her over the couch, pulling down her jogging pants. Realizing he was right about her not having on any panties.

"I knew yo freak-ass didn't have no drawers on." Mesha just laughed.

Soulja briefly admired the blessing of ass from behind, nodding his head and smiling. He noticed she was shaved down there just how he liked it. And with her legs, spreading the pussy was sitting there calling him like crack. He rubbed her outer walls then shoved a finger in her totally wet hole. inking to himself again that he could still get her wet with no work.

He slid slowly inside her, making her moan from pleasure. Soulja gripped her ass, spreading her cheeks apart. Slowly speeding his pace up until you could here their bodies smacking together from another room.

"Don't stop-don't stop. Baby I'm about to cum, "was all Mesha said before exploding on Soulja's dick and right while she was cumming, he was too. And together they fell on the floor.

"Go get a towel for me, Mesha."

"Okay, I'm still out of breath." Walking wobble-legged." Give me a second. When are we gonna get back together?" She asked, handing Soulja the towel.

I don't want to talk about that right now." Cleaning himself up and walking to the bathroom to finish. It was twelve' o clock when he checked." I gotta roll, but we'll talk "Okay?"

"Whateva, you say that all the time and we never end up talking about it."

"I said we'll talk." Soulja said, walking towards the door putting his gun at his waist." Tell the girls to call me, cause I promised to take them shopping this weekend,

"Okay-but damn, I want to go shopping, too." Mesha uttered.

"Yo ass don't need nothing, but , we'll holla later. I gotta roll, okay." "alright. I'll call you later."

Soulja called Special's cell phone from the car and told her he would be there in ten minutes, and asked her was everyone there.

"Yeah, they here waiting on you."

"I'm around the corner, so come to the door and pop me in." "I got you daddy, "She said before hanging up.

He pulled up in front of the club checking his rearview mirrors for the cops or the jackers, which was his usual routine cause he knew he wasn't immune to the wrath of the streets. Special was standing at the door with her gun in hand, waiting on Soulja to come in.

"It took you long enough."

"Whateva." He replied, smacking her on the ass while following her to the back. Sam was at the bar talking to someone. He and Soulja nodded at each other as they passed. Acknowledging one another's presence.

{The Crew}

The club was empty and it was and it was only noon in the middle of the week, so that's why Soulja wanted the meeting to be there. When he and Special walked in the back room, everyone he paged was sitting at the table. Lou and Tye, his top enforcers. L.C. who ran the out of Delaney Projects- whose pops was a banger in the 70s who killed a cop and get sentenced to life in prison- so L.C. was raised by the streets. He and Soulja clicked from day-one, so he moved up quick, from street rolling to running his own crew. But, everything came from Soulja. Tracy, who ran his own crew in the Bronx area of town- he and Soulja grew up together and been friends, forever tight. Steve had the east side of Glen Park on lock, but niggas from the west side had been giving them problems lately. Soulja and Special handled nothing but weight and kept close tabs on everything that was going on business-wise. Each crew had several crack-houses that were pushing a couple grand a night, but the cops were sweating tough lately cause of the increase in murders over the years. Everyone knew the Feds were somewhere in the city undercover, but these days they make their presence known hoping to make niggas in Gary scared to sell drugs and murder. But, it still went down daily.

"What's up, my niggas?" Soulja said from the head of the table. Everyone said what's up and then he got down to business, " I know there us money to be made, so I won't keep y'all long. But, I do need to know if there's any problem business-wise.

They all said things were good except Steve.

"Man, them niggas on the west side is starving since we opened up on the east side. So they been coming thru shooting on 39th. And the crib on the 41st last night"

"Y'all know where them niggas at?" Soulja asked.

"Yeah, we got all the info from one of them nigga lunching. We started to blast them fools but we wanted to holla at you first. We knew it was them because we saw the Monte Carlo with the busted windshield that came thru the first night, bombing."

"Close down those two houses." Soulja told them. "Why?" Steve asked. "Man, those cribs cranking."

"Cause I said so." Replied Soulja after what we put down on these niggas. I don't want it coming right back to our houses. Plus, we got two more houses out there. The fiends know where they are-so close the other two immediately."

"Alright bruh." Steve complied.

"Any other problems?" Soulja glanced around the room. "Well okay, let's get down to business."

Special gave him the gym bag with the dope in it. He opened it. Then laid it out the ten kilos it contained. This is ten bricks of coke that after being tested are uncut. So what were going to do is make 20 keys and have my ease the best dope in the city and probably in the state. Said Soulja

"A lot of niggas are starving right now cuz we keep that better work then them. But with this we gonna break a lot of hustlers pockets." said LC.

"We're gunna to really have to be on our shit. Cuz war may come with more than these Glen Park niggas." Said Steve

"A wise man once told me it ain't what you do its how you do it, and that it aint about how many people you kill but who you kill to get your point across." Said Soulja.

{Booby}

Soulja whispered to Special and told her to get Booby, code 47 ASAP. ~ at was his code for face-to –face, no phones. And as soon as possible.

Bobby was a real handyman because he gets the job done with no regrets or replays. He was a tall dark, skinny cat out of Chicago. Ill that Soulja met inside met inside the Lake County Jail few years back. Booby had crossed that border and came onto Indiana and was on his way through Hammond. IN to body some fool he wasn't into it with. But for some reason the cops got on him and found this old boy with two .50 cals in the car. Already a felon, he was charged with felon in possession of a handgun and was denied bond. While Soulja was locked up on one of his few murder charges that wouldn't stick because the witness wouldn't come to court, so they always got threw out. The two of them met in VB at the county and they became real tight, quick. Booby would let Soulja how he got down, and Soulja would tell him that he watched too much TV. Because half the shit he said was really made for television. But Booby was for real.

Booby got the page and smiled because he knew somebody was about to die. He didn't know whom , nor did he care why, but he knew by the page that somebody was going to die.

{THE MEET}

~ ey met up the next day at the truck stop off I-94 and Burr Street in Gary. When Booby walked in, Soulja was already at his booth in the corner where he could watch everybody before they could watch him.

Booby knew Soulja to be a real cautious cat and he liked that about him because slippers do count in this game they played.

"What up, my dude? Long time." Giving Soulja some dap. "Yeah. What's it been, like a year or more?"

"Damn! It has been that long hasn't it?" I guess the streets been peaceful for you for a while." Booby estimated. T e last time they saw each other Soulja had to get at some cats in East Chicago, Indiana. The Harbor area. Some boys came up real short on a pack, so Soulja sent a message by the name of Booby to make sure that never happened again- and it didn't.

Soulja explained the situation with the Glen Park cats that keep shooting up the crib out there, and that his people found where these old boys lay. He wanted Booby to handle it quietly because the streets were hot. And you can't get money and war at the same time while the cops are everywhere.

"My people can take care of this shit. But, they don't give a fuck. Man, all they wanna do is roll over there spray everything moving. And have the whole block on the news or some shit. Which I damn –near said go ahead, but naw, I want this don. quietly. Feel me?"

"I got you big homie. Just give me the info."

Soulja slid Booby an envelope with $10, 000 inside with the information he got from his people, then he dapped Booby and walked out.

[Carlos]

"Hey Carlos!"

"What the fuck man, can't a guy get his dick sucked in peace anymore."

"Sorry bro, but we got problems, said Juan.

"I don't give a fuck, bro I told you to stop bursting into my office." Carlos pulled his pants up then smacked Jamie on the naked ass which was peeking from under her mini skirt." I'll get with you later, mami." Okay papi-call me." The Puerto Rican and black girl replied, with long black hair that reached her waist and a beautiful pair of tits to go with the perfect ass.

Carlos found her swinging on the pole when he first was sent to Miami three years earlier by the bosses in Cuba to run things there.

"One of these days you're gonna bust in here and I'm gonna have your moms bent over my pool table, fucking the hell out of her." Carlos said.

"Hey man, that shit ain't funny motherfucker." Juan responded even though he knew Carlos was playing because they were best friends who came to Miami together.

"What's the problem, bro?"

"The fucking nigga in Indiana is dead, bro. Somebody killed him, and two of his boys a few nights ago, then burned' em up."

"What about my shit?" "Gone. Whoever killed him took it."

"You find who killed him, cause they owe me money. With interest." Carlos said.

"I'm already on it boss. I've sent some people to Gary to find the best dope around, cause it will be ours. You can step on that shit two, three times and have the best shit around here." Juan added.

"Yeah-I know. Keep me posted."

[Progress]

We found out that the victim in that fire was Michael Taylor, known on the streets as Slick, and two of his workers-Brandon Majors and Andre Walker. Slick has arrest for auto theft, burglary, and a weapons charge. The workers are full of petty juvenile arrest.' Detective Wilson stated."

"Narcotics say that Slick was coming up in the dope game real fast and maybe it was a stick-upon arrival crew needing him out the way."

"Yeah Wilson agreed." Medical exams show close range shots, execution style, and Slick even has one in the knee. e torture game was played here. This was a robbery."

"Let's hit the streets and see what we can find out." Detective Jones suggested.

[Po-Po please]

A couple hours later Special and Soulja were walking back to her car after getting taco's, but before she could pull off her car was surrounded by marked squad cars. She and Soulja were placed against the car and patted down. They had a female with them to search Special and her eyes got big when she pulled the baby nine out of Special's handbag. Soulja was clean at the moment.

"I got a gun here, "yelled the lady officer.

"I got a permit for that." Special stated with her usual attitude. She showed the permit and her I.D to the officer who took both of their info to the car to run them for warrants. Then an unmarked drove up and let Soulja know why he was being detained.

"Detective Wilson and Jones, y'all ain't got nothing better to do than harass taxpaying citizens". Soulja said.

"You probably never paid a tax in yo fuckin 'life." Detective Jones shot back.

"What y'all want, man besides to waist my time knowing they weren't arresting him because they'd been standing there to long.

'What you know about a burnt up drug dealer and a couple of his boys we found a few days ago?" Man I don't know shit about none of that, and won't know nothing next time I see y'all.' Soulja answered matter-of-fact." So can we leave? Our food is getting cold.

"What about you Christine?" Wilson asked, looking her up and down, but mainly at her hips trying to bust out her jeans.

"I don't know shit either."

"We gone get yo ass, Ronnie. One of these days you can bet yo ass on that one."

Wilson promised.

"Get the fuck out of here." Jones dismissed them. The detectives were really just finishing by messing with Soulja and Special. They couldn't stand him, that's why they bothered him-because they couldn't make a case really stick on him except that attempt murder that time, but he only did a few years and they wanted him gone forever.

"See, that's why I gave that one thang to Booby, cause of shit like that." Soulja referred to them getting messed with by the cops." That's why I told you to get that gun permit, or I'd be bonding that ass out right now." He added.

"Yeah, but you'd bond this ass out tho.' That's all that matters." At that time Soulja's phone was ringing.

[Bad Tony]

"Hello? What happened Baby? Let me speak to yo momma.... What's up Mesha? He did what in front of my kids?" See that's what I be talking about with yo ass fucking with these nothing ass niggas." Where he at now?" aite man, I'll holla at you later. Soulja was pissed when he hung up the phone, and Special knew it too.

"What happened?" She asked.

"This bitch ass nigga, Tony who Mesha dealing with off and came by the crib today and they got into it about whatever and this weak as nigga put his hands on Mesha in front of my kids." Special knew Soulja loved his girls to death and still cared about his baby moms, but this was more bout the kids this time, because she deals with this nigga Tony.

"So, what's the plan?" Special asked.

"Go to the pool hall on the eastside. That's where the nigga at." Special was driving fast when they left the taco joint and she knew where he wanted her to go. When she pulled up, it was pretty packed for a hole in the wall pool hall. Soulja noticed Tony's grey Surburban parked by the door. Special took her gun out of her bag, hit the button under her glove compartment and a special door opened which contained a dirty baby nine that wasn't registered, so she switched them. He wasn't heated but was cool because he knew Special was. They walked in the door, and Soulja noticed Tony playing pool with a couple of his boys he hustled with.

Special dipped off from Soulja, making it look like he was alone. Then he walked over to the table next to Tony's and grabbed a pool stick. By the time Tony saw him, it was to late. He swung the pool stick overhand, breaking it on Tony's head, causing an instant gash to come to his head.

His guy went for his gun, But Special was too quick for him. Placing the nine to his temple, daring him to try her. She took his gun as Soulja beat the hell out of Tony, telling him don't ever place his hands on Mesha in front of his daughters. He left Tony bleeding and unconscious on the top of a pool table and walked out of a totally quiet building.

"You feel better now? Special drove away. "Not really."

"I got something for you." Special said. She went back to Sam's to retrieve the other car and headed home to get cleaned up and eat. "Looks like we'll be heating these damn tacos up, doesn't it?"

"Looks like it."

{Relaxation}

They made it back to the crib around nine that night and Special went and ran Soulja some bath water in their spacious hot tub bath. Soulja rested in the hot water soaking when a very naked Special came into the bathroom with two glassed of Dom P in her hand. Damn her body is right, he thought, accepting one of the drinks from Special.

She sat her glass down when she climbed in and went over to Soulja while he sat back getting his sip on. Taking his dick in her hand, standing over him, she slowly sat down on top of it.

Her pussy was wet and warm as it swallowed his dick up. She held his shoulders as she rode him slowly up and down, squeezing her pussy muscles on his dick, matching him stroke by stroke. Ten she turned around and rode him backwards so he could look at that ass better. He reached around her, playing with her pussy as straddled and playing with her nipples too. Making her cum several times. Soulja gripped both ass cheeks and rammed her faster and faster, making her moan out in extacy as they both came together in one final push.

Te sipped the rest of their Dom and chatted for a minute before they exited the tub.

"You got that deal tomorrow afternoon lined up?" He asked "Yeah, she meeting me at the mall in Merrillville at two-thirty." "You need me to roll wit you?"

"Naw, me and Candy going shopping anyway, so she gone roll with me."

Candy was Soulja cousin from Michigan City, Indiana and she was crazy as he was- if nor crazier. Her daddy was like a revolutionary mafucker who believed shit was gonna go down, and when it did he would be ready. He had every kind of gun you wanted or he could get it. Candy's pops made fully autos from semi autos. There was nothing this man didn't know about guns. And he taught Candy everything he knew. He taught all his kids about weapons.

Candy was a five foot, ten dark brown, sexy petite pretty muthafucker. Special 's always messing with her, saying stuff like look at America's next top model with a machine gun, and they would crack up.

"Hey, you took care of Milky the other day, didn't you?" Soulja said.

"Then that's what's up." Soulja got out the tub, tried off and went to his bathroom while Special sat in the tub thinking about Milky.

He'd been getting info from Milky for years, and just something about this time rubbed Special wrong. But he wouldn't touch Milky without Soulja's okay. She got out the tub, dried off and went into her room where she oiled herself down and watched her big screen plasma TV until she fell asleep. ~ey never ate tacos.

{REAPER}

As Antwon was pulling up in front of his crib in his Yukon with the 26-inch rims, he was laughing to himself about how he just left Tamika thick ass naked and sleep at the hotel, with a mouth and ass full of nut. She gave great head and liked to be fucked in the ass. *Damn.* He thought about going back. *But fuck that gold-digging ass bitch wit her stankin ass always at the club baller-chasing.* ~ that's why he left her at the room-cause she aint shit, was what he told himself. *She better be lucky I left her a twenty for the cabin the morning.* He walked up to his front door, still buzzing off the Remy from the club. And as he opened his front door he noticed it was kind of dark in his crib. But he shook it off and walked on into the living room to hit the light switch. The floor cracked a lot like he was walking on paper or something, so he made it to the switch and hit to see everything wrapped in plastic. The floor, furniture, TV, everything.

When he looked up, in walked a guy with dark clothes, dark boots, rubber gloves, and a pair of fucking safety glasses on, who was carrying a nine millimeter with a silencer on the end of it. Antwon couldn't say a word, he just froze.

"I hope you don't mind- u drunk the last of the orange juice." He shot Antwon dead center in the forehead and watched him fall to the plastic. He then took out his pad and scratched off one of the three names on his list, wrapped the body up never to be found and *whoosh.* He was gone like the reaper.

{Candy}

The next day was Saturday and after Special got dressed in her baby-blue Phat Pharm outfit She grabbed two bricks of coke and put them in her stash spot in the trunk, then headed to pick up Candy. She still laughs when she thinks about when Candy's boyfriend tried to break up with her because she was scared of her. She broke his jaw with some brass knuckles and set the house on fire with him inside. Special asked her why she burned the house down and she said she was showing him how to end a relationship. They laugh about it every time they got together.

Special tossed in her Keisha Cole C.D. and then called Candy. "What's up, girl?"

"Hey hoe," yelled Candy through the speaker phone.

"I'm on the highway right now. I'll be there in bout fifteen minutes, so be ready."

"Whatever bitch. I told yo ass about calling me on speaker phone."

"Hoe, be happy I called and didn't just pull up in front of yo crib blowing the damn horn, pissing yo neighbors off. Cause yo ass aint never ready. "

"Whatever. I'm ready, girl."

"Aiight." Special said hanging up the phone. Then she turned up her song, 'Sent From Heaven'

Candy put on a tight fit-blue jean skirt outfit t, grabbed her sun glasses, her black bag, black shoes, and her black .389 automatic. They won't give her a gun permit for some reason and she had no felonies on her record. Every time she goes to the police station to fill out for a permit, they tell her to get out. So, she just carry her shit anyway.

Special pulled up and Candy jumped in. Immediately they hit the streets. Special was to meet Tito's girl at the mall in 45 minutes, she was coming to get two bricks from Soulja who always let the ladies handle the transactions. Plus, Soulja and Tito had been doing business for about a year, once a month or month and a half.

Tito was from Detroit. He and Soulja met in a club down there and exchanged numbers and just hit it off like that. Soulja told him about the dope he had at the moment and Tito had to get two bricks of it. Tito had to have twenty five a piece to get it as it was, untouched. So, he sent fifty grand with his lady to meet Special at the mall.

The transaction was made at J.C. Penny's dress department. Tito's girl would go in the clothe room and leave the money while she tried on some bullshit outfit. Then Special would go in and get money, leave the bricks and be out. The ladies never spoke.

"Why y'all meet in that cheap ass store?" Candy asked while waiting outside J.C. Penny for her girl.

"I don't know. Maybe that's the bitch favorite store to shop at." Special replied. They both broke out laughing.

"Let's go get a cinnamon roll from Cinnabon."

The two strolled through the mall catching all the eyes of the men and the women, too. Special's ass just rotating hard from left to right and Candy with those long, mouth-watering legs strutting her stuff. Too bad the fellas didn't know that these were some dangerous bitches who played for keeps.

{Chill Time}

Soulja was pulling up to Mesha's, dropping the girls off from shopping like he'd promised. He looked at his watch and it was 5:30 p.m. He, Big Tye, and Lou were supposed to meet up later and hit the strip club to have a couple drinks. He didn't speak to Mesha that morning when he picked up the kids because he was still upset she had that nigga, Tony all up under his girls and she know that nigga aint shit. He grabbed some of the many bags they had and went towards the house where Mesha was in in the doorway.

"Hey Ronny, you could of spoke this morning when you picked the girls up."

"Yeah, I could have- but I chose not to." Soulja walked passed Mesha and to the living room to lay the bags down.

"Mamma, come look at what daddy bought us?" The girls yelled at the same time.

"Okay, okay." Their mother said.

Soulja kissed them and told them he'd call them later. Then he walked straight past Mesha without saying a word.. Soulja jumped in his car and called Tye.

"Hello!" Tye answered.

"What's good, family? We still on for tonight?"

"You already know I'm trying to see pussy and ass shaking." "Who driving?" Soulja asked.

"Let Lou drive. He act like he can't park the fucking Escalade since he bought it last week. And oh-yeah, he threw some sixes on it the other day. "Sweet."

"Aiight," Said Soulja. "Pick me up at the crib, like ten." "Got you big homie." Tye added.

"One." Soulja said before he hung up and headed for the crib.

{Let's Roll}

At 10:00 sharp his boys were outside and ready to hit the streets. Soulja had on a Roca Wear jogging suit with new Jordan's; everything red and white. With two pinky rings, matching bracelets, his A.I.T. chain with the diamond cut, and a freshly oiled-up, shaven head. Big Tye had on a Sean John outfit. Puffy may have given him personally because you won't find it in any store you go in- with rocks shining from his ears and neck. Lou had on Pelle Pelle, with his Rolex watch and studs in both ears. ~ These boys were shining fasho in Lou's blue '08 Caddy Escalade on chrome sixes.

"Where we going, Shang?" Lou asked Soulja.

Shangrala was a strip club in the Miller area of Gary that kept a nice assortment of ass to choose from. But, Soulja's baby worked there. Her name was Chrissy, B.K.A. Dime Piece that was bad, had young dark brown, pretty face, big tits, pretty eyes and long hair. With a nice handful of ass that Soulja loved to squeeze on.

He met Dime Piece when she was 19 and he was working security at Sam's one night. A party was going on. She came to the door with two friends and asked Soulja did they need any dancers. He plugged her with Sam, and him and her been messing around since.

There was a nice crowd of cars when they pulled into the lot and parked. All eyes were on them when they walked through the door shining like new money. Fifty Cent's *Disco Inferno* blared through the speakers as a girl named Sensation wrapped her legs around the pole and slid down it with her legs spreaded wide open so you could see how fat her pussy was under her g-string. Guys were throwing bills onto the stage as well as on top of Sensation. Girls were walking around the club in their little skirts with ass hanging out, trying to get guys to buy private dances from them.

The fellas found a table by the wall so they could peep out what was going on all through the club. They ordered some Hennessey shots from the very fine red-bone waitress who took their order. As Soulja glanced around he saw Dime Piece at the table with like four cats-her and went to his table, making the guys she left very upset.

"What's up, Daddy?"

"What's good, lil mamma? I see you chasing that paper as usual." He commented.

"You know me better than anybody in here. I gotta get paid." Dime Piece told him. "So, you gone buy a dance tonight"

"Girl please, you know me better than that. I can get the whole combo after the club. What I'm gone pay for a piece now for?"

She knew Soulja didn't do lap dances, but she felt like messing with him anyway. He always tipped all the girls, well when he came because he respected their hustle and loved to see them dance. He'll be good to tip close to 1, 000 before he leaves.

Tye seen the one he wanted though, and she went by Mocha. A five foot five inch goddess that weighed 145 lbs with a flat stomach, wide hips, and an ass you sleep on. It was so big and soft, with her chocolate skin, shoulder length hair and Halle Berry sized titties. *Damn this was a bad Bitch.* Tye bought a couple of dances from Mocha and a couple of drinks which he would later call a small investment into the lady's stocks and bonds.(Well, actually her ass, pussy, and them lips.)

Lou was just a flirt. He was trying to bang all the women in the club and damn near did, with his cool game running ass. They drank, laughed with the girls over that loud ass music until around 2:00 then they left the Shang and all headed in drunk ass hell.

"Soulja, we still rolling down to Nashville next weekend?" Lou asked.

"Yeah man. I'ma take ya'll to the Marage and let ya'll see some real pussy and shaking."

That's what's up." Tye cut in.

The Shangrala on a good day might have fifteen girls, and they are not allowed to get butt-naked in Gary. The Marage in Nashville, on a weekend might have close to 100 bad black women in there getting asshole naked, putting that pussy in yo face and some on ya dick if your money and ya game right.

Special's Monte Carlo was parked outside when they pulled up, and for some reason he bet she was at the window with her gun. Making sure he made it in the house safe. And he was right because before he put his key in the door, she opened it – gun in hand. In some pink footies and pink panties that slid up her crack, and a pink tee.

He went to the living room and flicked the plasma ON and sat on the couch, kicking his Jordan's off . "How did things go wit Tito's girl today?"

"It went as planned." Special replied

"What's up wit Candy crazy ass, she still can't keep or find a man?" Laughing at his cousin.

"I'll make sure u tell her that." said Special on her way to bed. "Goodnight, boy."

"Goodnight ma." Soulja watched her ass eat up her panties as she walked away. He instantly got a hard, but he was a drunk so he pushed the thought away and went to sleep.

{Number Two}

On the other side of town, Reggie was walking in the crib after a great day at his drug house. He sold out twice, so he called it a night. Shit, it was like 3:00 in the morning so he figured he'd put his loot up, take a bath and chill for the rest of the night.

They'd been calling Antwon all day and still couldn't get him. They figured he was laying up somewhere and they were right. Partly.

Reggie was in the tub watching the TV his baby momma had put in the bathroom so she could bath and watch her storied at the same time. Reggie told her that was dangerous to have over the tub like that, but since she moved out it came in handy, She he left it there.

Halfway asleep, Reggie was awakened by a skinny cat in black. With rubber gloves on and some damned safety, glasses, holding the TV over the tub. Before Reggie could make a move..,

"You know this dangerous, don't you?" Then he dropped the TV into the tub with Reggie, ending his life. It would be later ruled an accident and case closed.

The man took out a pad and scratched out the second name on his list of three. - en he vanished.

{Juan}

Carlos' people had been in Indiana for a few days now, trying to find the dope and whoever killed Slick. Juan never really liked Slick, he felt Slick was weak. But Carlos saw his eagerness and drive to make money, so he gave the dude a chance .

Slick had met Carlos in Miami a year and a half earlier when the streets of Indiana, Chicago, and Detroit were dry of coke. One of Slick's cousins in Miami had a gun in Carlos' organization who owed him a favor, so he plugged Slick after the cousin vouched for him. Carlos had been searching for more reliable people outside of Miami to move weight because he could get as much as he could move.

This package Slick just got was his third re-up and this was a front to be paid for later. That's why Carlos was pissed. Because he hadn't been paid yet and Slick was putting together a chain of constant buyers from Chicago and Detroit. So Slick's death cost Carlos a lot of money that he planned on getting back from the people who killed Slick.

"What have you heard down there?" Juan asked his guy Tony, one of the men he sent to Indiana.

"So far it's quite, but we're on it."

"Did you set the meet with Slick's people there tomorrow?" Juan implored.

"Yeah. They'll be at the warehouse at seven like you said." "Okay." Juan said. "I'll be down there tomorrow." "Alright Boss." Tony hung up the phone.

Juan felt he needed to make sure that one of Slick's own people didn't burn him for the come-up, so he set a meet with the rest of Slick's crew with something to gain by hitting him.

{Attention Everybody}

The next evening when Juan walked into the warehouse there was ten of Slick's guys there, but Juan came in three, 600 Benzes, an Expedition, and a Yukon totaling 18 guys with automatic weapons. Slick's next-in command was his man Troy who moved to Indiana from Chicago five years ago when he and Slick got to getting real money together. He was a big fella who looked like he needed to be playing pro football, standing 6'4" and weighing 260 lbs. solid. Troy did time before and just kept the weight on by staying in the gym hitting that iron.

"I don't like to fly." Juan said. "Neither do I like to be in a fucking car all fucking day to come to this shit hole from my nice house in Miami. But I had to because your guy is dead and out shit is gone. My first question, Troy, is how do I know you or none of these guys double-crossed Slick and took my shit for yourself-huh?"

Troy stood his ground and Juan liked that deep inside. "Man, I aint no fucking snake. Slick was my guy, and there some real cats we got around us. We don't get down like that."

"Troy- ok then, where the fuck is my shit? Juan asked, looking around the very quiet room. Getting no answer, he said it again. Raising his voice louder the second time. "Where the fuck is my shit?" Then he pulled his chrome .357 Dessert Eagle from his waist and shot Troy in the chest twice, killing him instantly.

All you heard in the room was the cocking of Juan's guy's automatic weapons as they surrounded Slick's terrified boys. Juan really did believe Troy, and he actually liked him better then Slick. But he had to make his point and he really didn't like the fact this fucking nigger wasn't scared of him.

One of Slick's guys said a chick he messed with saw Slick at Shaw's the night he was killed with this stripper named Milky and some chick he never seen before. She told him that the chick. Milky, be on that set-up shit. We been looking for her, but she disappeared after that and nobody seen her anymore.

"Put a twenty thousand dollar reward out for the bitch. Somebody know where she at." Juan took his card and gave it to the kid and told him to call. He wasn't leaving Indiana until this shit was resolved.

So, the other guys in Slick's crew went to strip clubs in Gary and Eat Chicago where Milky was known to have danced. They let some of the girls know about the twenty grand for Milky;s whereabouts. Those hoes turned into pussy detectives trying to get that 20K. If she turned up there was no doubt the word would get back with these gold diggers in the case.

(Back to the Money)

"Man that new dope got these feigns going crazy for that shit."

"Yeah man, I aint been to sleep yet cause of the traffic at the door." Lil Man replied.

"Shit, I got ten left and that's another thousand-count."

"I'm down to eight myself. Didn't you call Tye for the re-up?" He asked Tracy.

"Yeah, he on his way."

"Ah shit." Lil man said as he peeped out the window. "What's up?" Tracy wanted to know.

"Here come that bitch Lacy wit all that ass. An I bet that bitch broke and beggin." He added.

Lacy was a redbone dime-piece turned dope fiend after this dope boy she was dealing with started getting high. He talked her into trying the shit and she's been sucking on the pipe ever since. And the most fucked up part is the nigga who turned her out got clean and back on his money and left her in the streets lost. That's been two years. Yet the shit hadn't destroyed her yet because she was still thick as hell and cute whenever she wasn't looking like she's been up for a week chasing rocks in the same clothes. A nigga who didn't know her would try to wife her in a minute, and then he'd probably kill the bitch three months later for selling his TV for crack.

"Lacy only twenty three years old and fucked up like that." Tracy looked at her through the window as she walked up the stairs to the door.

"I hope she don't have no money." Lil Man said. "I've been wanting to hit that for a while now"

"Man we working." Tracy reminded him. You know the rules, nigga. Keep you eyes open at all times and stay focused." Soulja had rules for all the houses to keep shit being ran tight with no mess ups.

"Man fuck that." Lil Man said. "We been here all night getting money for that nigga, so I'm bout to keep my eyes on Lacy's ass hole I focus on bussing this nut. You telling me you don't want none of that?" Pointing at her standing on the porch.

Tracy had to admit that today was one of her good days. Lacy had her hair freshly French braided beck in some tight, white booty shorts with a white t-shirt and no bra. You could see those hard ass nipples bussing through her shirt. She knew what she was doing when she put that outfit on because she didn't have no money at all. Lacy didn't really like trading sex for drugs but she wanted to get high by any means.

Usually she would try to run game first and use sex as a last resort because she was still a bad bitch and felt the world was beneath her. But once she stuck that pipe in her mouth she lost all the respect she carried as a bad bitch in the streets.

"What's up, Lacy?" Lil Man said as he opened the door.

"Lil Man, let me get a bag til I sell these food stamps later on an I'll bring it back." He knew he had her then because he could see the desperation. And he was loving it inside.

"Naw man, I can't do it." Lil Man said, acting like he was about to close the door on her.

"You wanna do something then?" She offered, "For a couple bags?"

"Tracy in here. Come on. " He left Lacy inside the door and went to the other room Tracy was in.

"You want some of this?" Lil Man asked his guy.

"If Tye pull up and catch us on his shit, our add us hit bra." "Well, let's hurry up then."

No fiends had been to the door in the last fifteen or twenty minutes, making things real quite inside the Bronx crack house. A little too quite if they would've been on point. After making the deal for the both of them to fuck Lacy, they took her into the living room and told her to get naked.

First, she peeled off her t-shirt, showing off her rock-solid nipples on her firm, handful of tits. Then she slowly pulled down her booty shorts, fighting to get them over that perfect round mountain of an ass. Lacy was clean shaven, showing her clit piercing which hung down from that fat, bald pussy. All she had on were her socks and gym shoes.

Tracy sat down on the couch and unzipped his pants and watched as she stuck her hand down his pants, pulling out his hard dick. Lacy got her down on her knees onto the carpeted floor taking Tracy's dick into her hot mouth. Leaving her ass hanging in the air with her legs spread, showing off her naked pussy to Lil Man.

He got down onto his knees behind Lacy after putting on a condom, sticking his dick into her already wet pussy. Lil Man held on to her hips as she slowly went up and down on Tracy's dick. Taking him deep into her tonsils, jacking him off at the same time and he was in heaven while Lil Man started pounding the woman from the back. Feeling the nut building up in his sack getting ready to explode.

{Bad News}

His dope was in his pocket and Tracy's dope was in his pocket while the 12-guage pump was laying on the floor on the floor by the door when the hinges were knocked off by the ram from the S.W.A.T. Team, raiding the Bronx crack house.

Big Tye had just turned the corner when he saw the spot being hit by the S.W.A.T. and his guys begin to lead the paddy wagon in cuffs along with that bitch Lacy with the fat ass. There was a hidden drop box in the floor for the dope and money in case of emergencies like this, but Tye hoped these niggas wasn't in there tricking with that bitch and got caught slipping. He pulled out his cell phone and called Soulja.

"What up, Tye?"

"The Bronx wall collapsed." Letting Soulja know the house got hit. "I'm on it." Soulja confirmed.

"One." Tye left out the part about the girl because he knew Soulja was gone be pissed off if these niggas were tricking on duty.

Soulja got on the phone with the lawyer, Larry Davis, and let him know what was up. Davis was a bad motherfucker in Lake County, constantly winning cases out there. He was retained for these types of situations. Davis told Soulja the men would be put on a 72 hr hold called P.C, then either charged or released. It depended on what they were caught with.

Soulja hoped they used the drop box, but would soon find out they got caught with a total of 18 dime rocks together, plus a total of five grand in cash. With five marked 20 dollar bills in the bunch. Soulja had Lou to call all the other houses and tell them to shut down for the rest of the day and reopen in the morning to be safe.

Three days later the lawyer contacted Soulja and told him that Tracy and Lil Man were in the County jail. They both had possession of controlled substances and dealing charges because they found the dope and money on them. Their bond was $6, 500 a piece cash or $65, 000 surety bond.

He was pissed when Davis told him that there was a girl arrested with the name of Lacy Robison and she was charged with visiting a house of common nuisance-a misdemeanor meriting a three hundred dollar bond. Soulja knew Lacy real good, he used to serve her boyfriend weight a few years back, and use to see her fine ass on his passenger's side looking good as ever. He heard she fell off and started smoking. What a waste, he would say. Now he knew why they got caught with the shit-they were tricking with that bitch.

"Send Tracy's mom with the money to get him. Since she's a nurse it won't look funny, But Lil Mike we gone use the surety bond, and bond Lacy out, too if she still there when ya'll go get them niggas." Soulja said." I feel kind of sorry for her, she had potential, and tell her to give me a call."

[Close Call]

As L.C. was closing the crack house early in Delaney Projects after receiving the call from Lou, he barely made it off the block, before the County S.W.A.T Team drove down the street and stopped in front of the house. They went and raided the empty crack spot.

When Soulja heard about that, he felt someone may have been dropping dimes in the five-o ears about his spots. He knew something was up and he had to find out because he'd just lost two money houses and didn't like what was happening.

Soulja had Lil Man and Tracy brought to Sam's when they bailed them out. He, Special, Lou, and Tye were there when the two of them came into the back room. They just stood there looking stupid when Soulja asked them how they could get caught with the money and the dope with a drop box right there in their faces. He knew the answer, he just wanted them to man-up about it.

'We fucked-up.' Tracy started. And got to fuckin with that bitch Lacy."

"See man, that's why there's rules to prevent shit like this from happening."

Explained Soulja.

"I'm sorry." Lil Man apologized.

"Yeah, me too." Soulja said. en Lou put the silencer to Lil Man's temple and pulled the trigger. He was dead before he touched the ground.

Soulja found out from the lawyer that Lil Man had talked to detectives several times, asking to talk while he and Tracy were in the county. Lil Man tried to get a deal because he knew they were facing prison time, but Tracy stayed like Soulja expected.

"keep ya dick in ya pants at work." was all he said to Tracy and then walked out the room.

[Milky]

Special gave Milky fifty grand of the lick from Slick and she got the rest of her stash and went to Atl. She didn't know there was a bounty on her head because she hadn't been in touch with anyone since she left. Plus, she had no real family in Gary anyway. Just the couple of girls she danced with.

Milky had been partying her ass off in Atlanta, and she found a nice little pad to rent. She'd been meaning to call her girl Luscious who danced with her in Gary. She knew Luscious would wanna come down there and dance at some clubs in Atlanta and make some real good money, because she was a brown skinned brick house with a six pack stomach, light brown eyes, calve muscles that made her thick thighs look even better, with a fat ass and huge tits. She and Milky were tight and had talked about going to the ATL.

Milky glanced at her watch, which let her know it was 11:00 in Gary, and Luscious would be at work. So, she called her cell phone, catching Luscious in the dressing room smoking a joint with another dancer named Heather. A snake in a thong. is bitch would steal from her mother and everybody else.

"Hello, Luscious answered, passing the weed to Heather." Hey Milky! Girl, what's up?"

Heather's eyes got real big when she heard Milky's name. She almost choked on the weed. She was in the club the day Slick's guy said that about the twenty grand for Milky, but Luscious wasn't .Today was her first day back. Luscious had been out of town on family business.

"You where, bitch?" That's what's up. Hell yeah I'm for that!" stated.

"This your number? Okay, I'll call you at the end of the week, okay. Bye girl."

They hung up.

Heather was plotting since she heard Milky's name." What's up with Milky?" She asked. "I ain't seen her around lately."

"She cool." Luscious stated." Getting that money as usual."

"Where she dancing at now?" Heather tried for gold, but Luscious knew the bitch was nosey as hell.

"She bouncing clubs-you know how we do it." Luscious replied.

Damn! Heather thought. T en she tried one more thing. "Can I use your phone to call the crib right quick?"

Luscious felt that this bitch was up to something, she just didn't know what. So she let her use the phone. And while Luscious wasn't paying attention, she went to INCOMING CALLS and remembered the last call. Then acted like she didn't get an answer and gave the phone back. Heather wrote down Milky's house number, got dressed and left work early. She knew one of Slick's workers so she went to where he got money at, which was behind her aunt's crib in Miller.

She seen him and had someone go get him. She asked him if the twenty grand was for real for info and he said hell yeah. He tried himself to get the info from her, but she wouldn't budge. So, he made the call to Juan.

Juan personally met Heather and asked her how good the info was. "This is where she lives at." She told the man whose eyes scared the hell out of her.

He could tell she was scared and that made him believe herm so he took the number and gave her the money.

Juan was a handsome guy of thirty years old who stayed in shape and dressed the part of a player. He was well groomed but his eyes showed a lot of death and pain in them. From the early days in Cuba when he killed and watched people he loved being killed. He made a phone call and gave the person on the other end of the line the number and then he hung up.

The next morning his hotel phone rung and he pulled out a pen and pad after telling whoever it was to hold on. He wrote down the info that the person on the phone gave him then he hung up.

He picked his hotel room phone back up, said a few words then hung up. A few minutes later he had a knock on the door in which he answered to one of his men. He grabbed the paper he wrote the info on them gave it to his man.

"This is where the bitch at in Atlanta, Georgia. Go get her." Juan said. "I have a few questions for her to answer."

{It's the weekend Baby}

"Man, the way shit been going this week, I know you aint still tryna roll down to Nashville tomorrow. Are you bra?" Lou asked.

"The Bronx spot is dead, Tracy looking in the area for another replacement as we speak. L.C. closed the one they hit down but opened up on the next block the next day. So we good in the projects and we gone open back up in Glen Park this weekend. So, hell yeah we still going south tomorrow. Special can handle shit here til we come back Sunday night ir Monday morning." Soulja explained.

"Am I gone drive the Lac truck?" Lou asked, wanting to take his new toy down south.

"Naw lil brother. I got this one." Soulja told him.

"You driving the Q all the way down south." Tye explained because they knew that was Soulja's only car because he didn't really care about rides like that. But, he loved his Infinity.

"Naw man, not the Q." Soulja said, keeping them in suspense.

"Then what?" Lou asked him. "Y'all will see tomorrow."

The next day Special took Soulja, Tye, and Lou to pick up their transportation for down south. And Special didn't even know what it was, and she knew everything. She pulled up to the detail shop and they were all standing outside her Monte Carlo when the owner pulled up next to them in a pearl white, spankin' new H2 Hummer on thirty-inch Asanti rims and tossed the keys to Soulja then went back inside. Special, Tye, and Lou all tripped off that truck.

"This muthafucker came wit a tour guide, but I gave her back" Soulja said. "I got the extra chrome down the side, the special-made Hummer grill in the front, the fifth thirty-inch rim on the back, two sunroofs in the top, TVs in the headrest, the steering wheel, and the flip-down with the video games for you kids." Pointing at Tye because he loves those games. "White leather seats wit black trim, wood grain interior... Shit" Said Soulja.

"What's up ?" Soulja asked?

"Remind me Monday to go back and get the tour guide, cause this shit takes too long." They all busted out laughing.

"Check this out." Soulja tapped on the windows." Bullet proof." " This nigga think he Fifty Cent or somebody.'

"Fifty aint doing it like this." Soulja answered, hitting a latch three ways next to his center console. The whole unit slid forward and up came twin Colt 45s with pearl handles holstered next to each other with ten round clips next to them.

"Damn, that's gangsta!" Special exclaimed. "Fuck Fifty Cent." Lou said.

"Let's roll." Tye added.

Soulja had his last words with Special, making sure that end was tight, but he knew she was good though. Special didn't want him to go but she knew boys would be boys, and told them to be safe.

The fellas jumped into the truck. Lou got up front and Tye got back so he could play Madden on the flat screen. Soulja jumped on 65 South and they were on their way. He put in Tupac, So many tears, and said, "Oh yeah-I forgot." Then turned the volume up. Tye and Lou both said damn while covering their ears from the loudest, most clearest sounds money could buy. 2 Pac sounded like he was in the trunk with a mic.

"Cut that shit down some!" Tye yelled from the back seat." My heart gone mess around and stop." Looking back at the system Soulja had installed in the H2.Everything was competition.

He had like ten subs in bricks of two's. With an amp for each set of two's. Speakers were in the walls and doors, plus tweeters in all the corners. Two different amps pushed his highs and a couple powerful crossovers. The set up looked like some shit straight out of a low rider magazine. "How much you pay for all that shit?"

"Twenty grand."

"For a muthafucker who don't really like to floss, you show know how if you do."

Lou commented.

They pulled in to Nashville, Tennessee around 7:00that evening and went to the three rooms at the Ramada. Soulja told his guys to be ready to roll about 9:30. He wanted to rest up then get changed up because tonight they were going to Louie's club.

[Louie]

Soulja met Louie, a time he came down here before and they did business together. Louie owned a hot night club that be poppin' on the weekend, so Soulja figured they would go there first because the strip clubs are opened until five in the morning.

At 9:30 the guys were at Soulja's door, clean as hell ready to roll because they had never been to Nashville. They were ready to party. Loui suits, Armani, Gators, and dobs; these brothers were clean. All of them iced

out-ears, necks, and wrist. They jumped in the truck and headed for the liquor store.

"Why you going to the liquor store when we going to the strip club later?" Tye asked.

"Because they B.Y.O.B. down here at the clubs."

"What the fuck is that?" Lou didn't understand the terminology.

"Bring your own bottle. You can take liquor to the club cause they only sell pop in the club, and the liquor stores close at like ten down here." Soulja pulled up at the liquor store and passed Lou a knot of money to get whatever.

Lou went in and got Remy, Hennessy, Crown Royal, and a case of Old English." I got money now, but I'm still hood. Believe dat." Getting back in the truck, passing Tye the drank to put in the back with him.

Soulja had called Louie, so he knew they were on their way. And when Soulja turned the corner to the club, it was poppin' on that street. It was July in the South, almost 80 at 11:00 at night. Women in the hottest dresses and skirts were walking up and down the sidewalk getting their flirt on with fresh hair dos and new gear. The ballers were out too, in some of the hottest whips. You seen BMW's rimmed out Lexus trucks, Mercedes, Caddy's-I mean a car show for real. But, it was all about the booty.

There was a line all the way down the block to get in the club, and as much as Lou and Tye were feeling the scene, they weren't feeling that line. That's because they didn't know how plugged Soulja was with the owner here.

Everyone was peeping the players out in the chromed-out H2 as it slowly crawled on them 30's down the street, shutting down all music when it rolled by bumping Scarface and Tupac's 'Smile'. Soulja pulled right up in front of the door to an empty VIP spot and the guy said, "Damn, you got it like that-huh." Everybody in the line wondered who these clean ass niggas were in the hummer with VIP status. They walked straight in the club and a couple gold-diggers were gonna make it priority to find out once they got inside.

Louie was a Puerto Rican cat of about 45 years old whose brother gave him the club ten teays ago as a gift. He was a little fat , bald dude who loved to trick with the young women.

"What's going on, my friend?" Louie asked, shaking Soulja's hand then speaking to Tye and Lou.

"I see you still keeping it jumping." Soulja commented on the crowd.

It was a very nice club with two bars, one in the front, and one in the back of the club. Big screen TV's played movies that you couldn't here because of the booming sound system. On weekends the local radio station D.J comes down to Louie's and host jams. It had a small dance stage in the rear and a huge one in the center of the building that stayed packed. He had couches everywhere, and two VIP sections.

Louie led the fellas to the VIP and had two Dom P. brought to their table by one of the finest waitresses in Tennessee. Her name was April, a light brown-skinned, five foot even angel with shoulder-length hair and dimples. The little skirt she wore hugged her cold, petite frame nicely.

"Will there be anything else?" She asked, smiling at Soulja as she sat the drink down.

"I'm sure I'll think of something.' He tipped April a 20.'So, don't get lost.'

"I won't, and thanks for the tip.'

The fellas sat back in the VIP, drinking Dom. Enjoying the stress free night of not being in Gary.

"This is what's up." Said Lou, pointing around the club.

"I see why you wanna buy Sam's and rebuild it." Tye agreed.

Yeah man, this is what's up.' Soulja watched all the fine women dance to lil Jon through the sound system.

Louie came back to their section and told Soulja he had something for him. Then, in came four country girls. Thick in all the right places. Since there was only three fellas, two of the ladies stayed with Soulja. They all laughed, drank and kicked it for a few hours and promised to get together tomorrow evening. They had business to take care of in the meantime, so Soulja gave one of the girls his phone number and told her what time to hit him. They hollered at Louie and then bounced.

It was three in the morning and they were still wired up and ready to part.

"Man, we gotta get with them before we bounce!" Tye said, fully enthused.

"Yeah, we do.' Soulja conceded." Man, if we going to the strip club, let's go change. Cause this may be to much for sweaty ass to be bouncing on top of. And I paid to much for this shit.'

'I feel that Lou added.

45

{Sweet}

The fellas went and changed into jeans and jogging suits with gym shoes, but they were in clean, top-notch gear. When they got to the Mirage it was jumping . You could hear the music in the parking lot. They grabbed the drank and went in the club. And when they walked in Lou said, "SWEET!"

There had to be fifty girls or more in thongs and booty shorts, just strolling around the club trying to get that money. And on the stage was a dancer named Passion with a tattooed cobra snake wrapped from her pussy all the way to her calve muscle. She was dancing to Mystical's 'Shake it Fast' and she was letting the whole world see it all.

When they walked through the door niggas were piled around Passion, tossing dollars on top of that naked pussy. The guys found a table and girls started swarming because they knew by what they wore and their voices, that they weren't from down south.

Soulja like this little, short brown-skinned brick house named Foreplay. He said she had a tip drill booty. And she did because baby girl was stacked. With a small waistline. There were so many women to choose from Lou started getting frustrated.

Tye has already talked a chocolate delight by the name of Shane into giving him some pussy in the lap dance room. She wanted $300, but he talked her down to half of that. He didn't care about the money, he would say it was dope fiend money any way-so fuck it.

The private room consisted of a bunch of couches in separate parts of the room with mirrors on the walls. Shane was from Memphis, Tennessee; fi ve foot, four weighing 135 with curves of a track and field athlete. Her frame was solid and that tight little ass and calve muscles protruded. She had on an all-red cat suit that was crotchless in the front and her ass cheeks poked out the back of it. Shorty was a ten fasho.

Tye gave her the money and sat back on the couch as the song 'Shake Yo Money Maker' came on. She popped that ass in Tye's face a couple times. Sliding her g-string over and bending forward so he could see that fat monkey. He put the rubber on and she sat on his lap like she was giving him a lap dance. Shane slid her g-string to the side with one hand and slid his dick in her pussy with the other hand and got to grinding up and down on his dick through two songs, until they both came. Soulja and Lou also ended up getting their thang on with a couple chicks who they plotted on.

The girls were clowning on stage in the Mirage Pussy poppin', making that ass clap, doing splits, you name it and they were making it happen there. The fellas were loving it and getting drunk at the same time.

"Man, we got to get out of Indiana more." Lou suggested with a red bone on his lap and a drink in his hand.

"Faho." Soulja agreed.

{Party's Over}

Milky was on her way into her apartment after leaving an Atlanta hot spot when she was ambushed at the door and given a shot that knocked her out . She woke up hours later dizzy as hell in the backseat of what appeared to be a Mercedes. Judging by the emblem on the seat. She was in the middle of two White or Mexican men in suits and there were two more up front.

At first she didn't know what the hell was going on. Then Milky remembered being ambushed at the door, being given a shot and passing out until the moment she awakened. She felt scared as hell because she didn't know what fucked up thing she did that had caught up with her ass. She'd done set up so many people and stole from men at every club she's ever worked at.

Milky wondered how long she'd been out, and then looked out the window. Noticing the sun up, she said to herself that there was at least four more hours of darkness when she got home. So she knew she'd been out over four hours. The captive peeked up and saw a sign that said Ind., and for some reason she knew her ass was in real trouble Milky just didn't know how much. Her hands were tied up and so were her feet.

The Benz pulled into the garage of an empty house owned by Slick. Then one of Juan's goons picked her up, tossing her over his shoulder and carrying her into the house. He took her into one of the bedrooms and sat her in a chair, tying her to it and then leaving her alone in there for like an hour.

An hour later Juan walked in wearing what appeared to be a painter's outfit with rubber gloves on and a scalpel in hand. He had one of his guys get him a chair and he sat in front of s terrified Milky who was crying and pleading on deaf ears.

"Now- I'm gonna ask you some questions." Juan said. "And your answers will determine how you die. Slow or fast. Cause yes, mami, I am gonna kill you today. You cost me time and money, and I hate that very much." He continued.

Milky still didn't know what this was all about yet. All she knew was that he was serious, and all she hoped was he would realize he had the wrong person and let her live. She felt hopeless under those conditions.

"Now- I wanna ask you about Sluck." Shit! T ought Milky.

{Juan}

Saturday evening Special and some of the guys were at Sam's when in walked ten Cubans in suits. And Sam said there were like eight more outside. Juan walked up to the bar and asked who was in the charge.

"I am." Sam stepped up. "I'm looking for Soulja." "About what?" Sam asked with concern.

Juan said a mutual friend told him that Soulja had something that belonged to him. Special came from behind the bar and asked, "What's that?"

"What business is it of your, little lady?" He said, checking her out.

"Anything that goes on around here is my business." Standing her ground, Special replied.

Juan seen strength in her, and he respected that as well as got pissed off behind the fact that a woman was sizing him up. He turned around and looked at one of his boys and started laughing, then said; "Now the bitched have all the balls!"

His cronies began laughing with him. Until Special drew her nine form her back waistband and pointed it at Juan's face. At the same time his boys drew the semi autos they had concealed, which made Sam draw the street sweeper from behind the bar. And the other two of Soulja's guys drew their weapons too. The only one unarmed was Juan.

"Now what, lil' Lady?" Juan asked her.

"I'm thinking about murdering a Cuban mothafucker wit a big mouth." Pointing her weapon at his face.

"You kill me, and then they kill you. And everybody's dead." He stated to Special.

"Look mami, maybe we'll get our chance to dance soon. But, right now you take this card on the table and have Soulja call me in the next twenty four hours- or we might dance sooner than expected." Juan continued, laying his card on the table then giving Special a small box. " This belongs to our mutual friend, and they would like Soulja to have it."

He gave Special the box then he and his crew mobbed out the club and got into Benzes and rolled out. She opened the box and instantly noticed Milky's ring.

"We got problems." Special said out loud. {Freaks only}

Soulja and the guys by this time done called up those four chicks Louie hooked them up with and they even brought two more of their home girls to the rooms. Soulja's room had the big Jacuzzi, couches , a couple beds, and a balcony. He and his two girls were in the hot tub sipping on Remy and Coke, listening to R. Kelly's '12 Play' on the radio. Lou occupied the twin bedroom where he threw his own porno or some shit. He had the chicks sucking each other's pussy from sixty nine position while he rammed whichever one was on top in her ass as the camcorder recorded.

Tye had a chick sucking his dick, Another one was sucking her pussy at the same time. It was going down in that room.

Soulja didn't even notice his phone ringing on silent mode in his pants pocket on the floor next to the bed.

{Game Over}

Brady called it a night after selling his last rock. It had been a good Saturday; except for he hadn't heard from Antwan and Reggie in a few days, He didn't care because he was cleaning up all by his self. Ever since they closed them niggas down, shit had been booming.

It was damn-near four in the morning, so Brady figured he'd find a 24-hour joint and get something to eat before heading in to his worthless ass baby momma. He really didn't want to be with her no more. But they

had a son together, so he kept her around and dealt with all the whining and bullshit. For the time being anyway.

He had to walk down the street to his car because you don't want to get your ride hot by parking in front of a crack house. As Brady got all the way up to his Chevy Caprice, he thought, the way I'm getting money now, I might go get that truck next week. Brady jumped in behind the limo tint. He started the car then set his mirror and almost screamed, but couldn't.

"I thought you'd be all night." The man with the safety goggles on said as he wrapped the cord around Brady's neck and took his life away from him in a matter of seconds. He then pushed Brady into the back and drove off fin the dead man's car.

Soulja and the guys partied with the chicks until the sun came up. He then sent them home. When he grabbed the phone from his pants pocket he saw that he'd missed a couple calls from a Special. And he'd received a text that read : MISSION COMPLETE. So, he knew Booby had handled business quietly. Soulja planned on giving him fifteen more grand when he got back to town.

{Drama}

It was early in the morning but he felt something was up with Special calling more than once, so he called her phone.

"Hello?"

"What's up ma? You sound wide-awake, and its seven in the morning down here."

"Yeah, I'm woke." Special said. "But listen, we got problems down here that need your immediate attention."

"That serious-huh?" Soulja said. "Yeah, that serious." She repeated. "We on our way."

"Aiight."

Soulja wanted more info but they didn't do the phone thang. But, he knew shit was real by the tone so he cut the trip short and jumped on the 65 North to Indiana. By that afternoon they were in the club getting the whole play-by-play about the Cubans and remembering the ring which belonged to Milky.

"How you know she dead if he didn't say she was?" Soulja asked.

"Because the ring is still on the finger." Special answered, giving him the box and showing him the card.

"Sam, did the outside cameras get their license numbers?"

"I'm already on it and waiting on a reply." They had a buddy who ran plates and got information for them.

"We got this cat's picture, too. On the inside camera. So, we gone find out who he is cause the card only got the hotel number." Sam made a call and came back to them and mentioned that the plates came back to an imports company in Miami, Florida.

"Alright Sam, fax this cat's picture to your people up that way and see what you come up wit." Soulja instructed. "And I'ma call em and see what's on his mind.

{Bad Deal}

"I got a deal I need to handle on the east side wit this old boy, Simeon." Tye said.

"He want a half a brick, so I'ma go handle that and I'll be back." He pulled out his baby, a 2006, 1300 red-and-white Kawasaki, because it was so nice outside. The boy could ride bikes like he was born on one. He did tricks, wheelies, and was a total speed freak. A rough rider. Tye put his helmet on, zipped up his Nike jacket and then made sure the dope was secure. He headed out to meet this old boy at the gas station on 21st and Delaware.

Simeon Bradley was a dope-boy Tye met through other people. This was only the second time dealing with him, and the first time was an eighth of a key. And two weeks later he wanted half a brick.

Tye seen him in his car parked by the pay phone and told him to pull up to the gas pump. He then went ahead and pulled up next to Simeon's passenger window where he would be out and not in. Tye never got off his bike or cut it off because something stunk.

Simeon put the money on the seat and Tye grabbed it and cuffed it quick because something seemed wrong. As he was throwing the dope into the car he noticed Simeon look toward the pay phone and the guy on the pay phone shook his head. At that very moment Tye knew it was a set up.

He hit that clutch, pulled that throttle and rocked out the gas station parking lot. At the same the FEDs were coming in from everywhere. Tye had the jump on them but the chase was on through traffic. Behind him four cars weaved in and out of traffic, passing regular cars and trying to catch up with the powerful 1300. Then, up front Tye saw two under covers coming straight for him, so he unzipped his Nike top with one hand. And as soon as he got close to the cops, pulled out twin Rogers while riding with no hands.

Tye crossed his arms, coming out the shoulder hoisters with 9 millimeters and opened fire on the unprepared police. Their cars riddled with bullets and they were forced out of his way. He then holstered his weapons and hit the corner so hard that he almost lost control of the bike. Experience made him hold on though.

The chase had been going on for almost twenty moments when Detective Wilson heard about on the radio. He knew Tye by name. Suspected in several homicides in Gary. Tye might have been involved in Slick's death also. According to an informant. The chase headed toward the detective's direction.

The highway was two blocks over, and if he could reach it, the police won't have a chance at catching him. The police couldn't get a shot off because he wouldn't be still long enough to give them a target. But, every chance he got, Tye pooped shots at their asses.

"This guy can ride!" One of the cops commented while trying to keep up.

Tye had did a complete circle. Now he was coming down the 25th Ave trying to get to the highway and had to be going close to eighty five when Detective Wilson pulled out an alley right by the highway clipped his bike. This sent Tye airborne, straight into a tree. He died before he made it to the hospital. Detective Wilson would be cleared of any wrong-doing in the death of Tye, but Soulja wouldn't forget. That shit was personal.

While the chase was going on with Tye. Soulja had called Juan and was at Sam's waiting to meet him personally.

"Hey Carlos!"

"What you got for me, Juan?"

"I found our friend in Indiana and I'm going to meet wit him right now. " Juan said from the back seat of his 600 Benz.

"Good brother. I knew you could handle this problem." Carlos stated. "But keep me posted."

"Alright bro" ~ ey concluded and hung up the phones. Then Juan made another call.

"Did you get the info? Good-good, then well go and pick the package up then come and meet me." Juan said before hanging up and lighting his Cuban cigar.

{Face to Face}

There were four other vehicles behind Juan's as he pulled up in front of Sam's club. But only he went in by himself this time.

"He's a cocky mothafucker, aint he?" Special mentioned about Juan's audacity.

On this Sunday afternoon the only people who were in the club were six of Soulja's guys. But across the street in the parking lot L.C. and seven of his guys sat in two Suburbans with dark limo tint. They were armed to the teeth with mini 14's, mac-11s, street sweepers, and Desert Eagles. Waiting on the sign and they'd come across the street bombing on everything alive on the sidewalk on which the Cubans stood.

Sam led Juan to the back where Soulja and Special was sitting at the table. Soulja shook the man's hand and told him to take a seat.

"Look, I don't fuck around wit games." Juan looked at him. "So, I'ma get straight to the point. I didn't like Slick, you see. I saw weakness in him. But my boss liked him. You killed him took fifty keys of cocaine from him

53

that belonged to my employer cause Slick hadn't paid him yet. So, that's why I'm here instead of being in my Jacuzzi getting my dick sucked." He glanced at Special and then back to Soulja.

"You took from my boss, now you owe him." Soulja said with a straight face, looking right at Juan. "I don't owe you employer shit." And who the fuck is Slick?" Standing his ground with the straight-faced Cuban.

"I know your girlfriend gave you the box from our mutual friend." Soulja thought about Milky's finger but didn't say anything.

"You see- me and Milky had a nice, long talk and I looked in her eyes and could tell she was telling the truth. And, she was even real sorry for what she did, so I forgave her before u cut out her heart." Juan continued. Soulja wanted to kill this dude bad as hell at that very moment. "So, please don't fuck wit me right now." said Juan.

"So what's stopping me from killing you now and having my boys murder your punk ass boys right now?" Soulja replied.

"You could do that, " Said Juan. "But for some reason I don't think you'll try it." One of his boys walked in and handed him an envelope, then walked back out.

"And why is that?"

Juan tossed the envelope in front of Soulja and said, "Welcome to the big league."

"What's this?" Opening the envelope and freezing as he saw photos of his two daughters. They were tied up and crying, Soulja drew his weapon and put it to Juan's forehead. He told him, "I'm gonna kill you if something happens to my girls!"

"They're fine, " Juan answered. "As of right now they are. So, put the gun up. You're wasting time." Soulja holstered his weapon and sat back in his chair.

"What do you want?"

"Slick owed my employer one million dollars and you have that debt plus interest, so we gone double that and give you one week starting right now." Juan stated the terms of their agreement although Soulja didn't willingly agree to it. "I'll be in touch" Getting out the chair and blowing a kiss towards Special on the way out the door.

"Fuck you!" She replied by giving Juan the middle finger.

Special knew Soulja was getting money, but she was for sure he didn't have no where near two million dollars. She doubted he had one million if he sold everything he owned.

"What we gone do?" Special asked Soulja, letting him know she had his back one hundred percent. He just sat there staring at the pictures of the kids, then wondered where their momma was.

He called her house but got no answer, so he and Special drove out to her crib. T e door was open so they went in guns drawn and found Mesha dead in the back room from a gunshot to the chest, Soulja's phone range. It was his enemy, Juan.

"Look at it this way. Now you won't have to pay child support." "I swear I'm gone kill you." Soulja told the abductor of his babies,

"Just get the money, tough guy. If you love these cute little girls." Juan hung the phone up on him.

Because of Mesha, Soulja knew he had to do the police thing. So, he gave Special his gun told her to take it off , he'd see her later. He went through the bullshit with the cops for the next six hours, telling those assholes to find his daughters because he didn't know where they were.

Even though they couldn't stand Soulja, not one of them believed he did this one. They let him go. On the way out he ran into Detective Wilson. ~ is detective didn't get Mesha's case, a Detective Marshall got it.

"Now you done killed your baby's mom." Wilson said. "Man, that's even below you."

"Go fuck yourself." Soulja walked past him.

"Hey, sorry about your buddy." Soulja still hadn't heard about Tye yet because of all the other shit going on.

"What buddy?" He asked.

"Your buddy Big Tye was in a shoot-out and high-speed chase today on his motorcycle and he crashed into a tree and died on the way to the hospital."

Wilson forgot to add that he pulled his car in front of Tye and clipped him. And the fact that that's how he crashed and was killed. But Soulja would find out later. He walked out the police station like 10:00 that night to one of his boys waiting on him out front.

"I can't believe Tye gone." Soulja uttered, knowing Tye gave em hell on that bike because he could ride his ass off .

When they got to Sam's everyone felt down. They'd heard about Tye and Sam let Soulja know about Wilson pulling his car in front of Tye's bike. ~ e mood was gloomy and bitter.

"This muthafucker the one who told me about the shit. But forgot to add that on." He planned on dealing with Wilson after all this other shit got taken care of. Sam, Lou, Special, and Soulja went into the back room and Sam came out with a pad.

"My Miami connects said the guy on the picture I faxed them is Juan Gutierrez, a Cuban nationalist over here in Miami working under a guy named Carlos Manilla. Also from Cuba. The bosses in Cuba sent Carlos over here to get a chain going to push coke through the states from Miami. Carlos' front is this import company. That's where the cars were registered, so we know where to find them." Sam continued. " They're a pretty big organization and we may need some help on this one if it comes down to it."

Special spoke up next. She said, "Look, we know how much you love those girls. So, the three of us came up with a little over three hunnit grand to help out."

"Thank yall. But wit that and my loot, I'm still gone come up like a mill short. And today is over, so I need to get a million dollars in six days." Soulja replied.

[Miami]

Carlos was having a get together at his mansion when Juan walked up to him at the pool area. Carlos had the bar maid get his guy a drink. He hugged Juan and they walked to a table by the pool.

Carlos kept a party going at one if his houses in Miami. This one consisted of thirty rooms, two garages, and a guest house with a pool and Jacuzzi. He also kept rappers and crooked politicians around. And, of course, an assortment of some of the baddest women in the city walking around in skimpy bathing suits.

"So, is our PROBLEM IN Indiana taken care of?" He asked.

"It will be in a few days?" Juan sipped on a drink that one of the women brought him.

"What do you mean in a few days?" Carlos began growing impatient with his friend .

Juan explained the whole play, and that he gave Soulja a week, and that he brought the girls back to Miami with him and they were staying at one of the safe houses they used to keep dope stashed in. Carlos didn't like the fact that Juan had done all this extra stuff without consulting with him first, but the ball was already in play, so let it roll while planning on having words with him once this whole ordeal was over.

"Keep me posted, "Carlos peered very seriously at his man.

"I got you bro." Juan really desired to be the boss. He wished the cartel would have selected him instead of Carlos .He felt like he did most of the work anyway. One day somehow he would be the man even if it meant killing his friend. He thought about it to his self while looking around Carlos' home. Smiling to himself. ~ en, all this will be mine.

Juan picked up his phone and called Tito at the safe house to see how his guests were doing.

Tito said, "Juan, what's up bro?" "How are my guests doing?" He asked.

"Besides crying-they're cool" Speaking about Soulja's daughters who were locked in a back bedroom with bars on the windows.

"I wanna go home!" Crystal yelled.

"Me too!" Marie added, looking out the window and seeing nothing but water from the beach.

This was a low spot on the beach where they stashed dope. A stash spot. It had no neighbors closer than a half mile.

"Don't worry Crystal, daddy gone come and get us." Marie consoled her sister." I miss mommy."

"Me too." Crystal agreed.

"Did you get them something to eat?" Juan asked. "Yeah bro. I got it taken of .'Tito reassured him. "Alright bro, call me if you have any problems.'

"I got you."

Juan didn't really like hurting kids, but he would to make a point. Soulja had six days left or his girls would die, he thought.

(On the clock)

Soulja had a little over seven hundred grand in cash stashed, and he received over three hundred thousand from Special, Lou, and Sam, which left him with six days to get one million dollars. It had taken him years to get at the spot he was at. He figured that even with all the houses pushing to the limit, the most he would pull from them in six days would be a little over a hundred grand, possibly.

Special advised him to be like fuck it, and go on a robbing spree hitting banks in back-to-back cities.

"Fuck it." Soulja didn't like that because he liked to peep shit out and have a plan before jumping off in some shit, but time wasn't on his hands this time, so he agreed." All we gone hit are the tellers." He knew the vault would take to long." And we need to be in-and-out.' No bullshitting.' Soulja's mind was made. Anything to save his girls. 'We go in the morning. You ready for this shit?" He asked Special.

"You know I'm with you until my breath stops."

He told Lou to watch over the houses and collect the money. Soulja told Sam to find out more about the Cubans from his people in Miami, and that he and Special could handle everything else but he would need a driver.

They chose Tommy who was one of Tracy's guys from the Bronx crew. He was an ex car-thief turned hustler. Back when he stole cars, he was gone in 60 seconds, and Tommy would get chased by the cops on purpose and never get caught. Soulja had him go and steal a nice, low car with speed if needed. So, he went out and found a four-door Chevy that had a 350 in it.

They hit the suburbs of Chicago first and found a nice sized bank called Federal Savings. It had just opened because it was early. It was good; it meant fewer customers to watch and contain.

They hit the door fast, Soulja in front wearing all black fatigues and a ski mask with the all black mini-14 and Special in tow with the same outfit and ski mask with a mac-11 semi automatic. He took the tellers by surprise. She caught security off guard, dreaming, and put him on the floor with the other four customers.

Soulja hit the counter telling them if someone hit the alarm or put a dye pack in the bag, he would kill all of them. He put all the tellers on the floor except one. To her, he gave the bag and rushed the lady from drawer to drawer. He'd chosen the youngest who was a white chick around about thirty years old.

Soulja checked his watch and he snatched the bag then ran out the bank and into the awaiting car with no problems, and a hunnit and fourty thousand dollars. Then they went boldly three blocks over and took Broadway Loans for another hunnit before dumping the car in the mall parking lot. here, Tommy stole a Tahoe and they were off again.

Things were going smoothly until they were leaving out bank number five in Milwaukee, Wisconsin named Bank One. A cop who just happened to be turning the corner at the time they were leaving the building saw a robbery in progress and radioed it in. He was not to engage the suspects until back-up got there, but the rookie wouldn't listen. He stopped in the middle of the street then jumped out his car- nine millimeter in hand- and yelled out, "FREEZE, " to Soulja and Special who were the two robbers pulled their weapon to open fire. The rookie got the first couple shots off first, his second round grazed Soulja's shoulder. Special noticed that he fl inched, so she knew he was hit, and that infuriated her as she squeezed off round after round. The mac- 11 riddled the cop car and blasted the officer center chest, knocking him to the ground.

"I'm okay." Soulja told her as they ran to their car to get away.

Back-up wouldn't make it in time to catch the assailants or to save the fallen patrol man.

{When it Rains it Pours}

This is a voluntary recorded statement made by Emanuelle Ortiz at the Hammond Federal Building and the witnesses are Federal Agent Gregory Hines Federal Agent Mark Watts and Homicide Detective William Wilson of the Gary Police Department. Please state your name into the microphone said Agent Watts. Emanuelle Ortiz. And you are currently employed by one Ronnie Parelli. The room grew quite waiting on the answer to that question. Remember your deal Mr. Ortiz, the only way you get immunity and witness protection are complete cooperation, or its face life in the federal prison. Now one again Mr. Ortiz are you currently being employed by Ronnie Parelli? Yes I am said Mr. Ortiz. Around three months earlier Mr. Ortiz was arrested trying to sell a key of cocaine to an under come officer and after searching him they found a nine millimeter with the serial numbers shaved off so to avoid the life sentence they kept throwing in his face he excepted a deal to give them Soulja in exchange for immunity and witness protection. The key he got caught with was a side deal Soulja didn't know about. He was trying to make some extra ends and got popped off in the process. By the time his interview was over four hours later the cops knew that Soulja, Tye, and Lou killed Slick and why. They knew about the Cubans from Miami taking Souljas girls, and soon they would know his last bank he planned to rob. This muthafucker gave them everything he knew and he knew more than most of the guys in Soulja's crew cause he been around. He told where the stash house was and where all the crack spots were. He told where Soulja and Special crib was even tho the feds new about that already. The only thing he didn't do was tell on Special he never said her name cause he always had a thing for her but her love for Soulja was about to go away, somewhere in his fucked up mind he thought he would be able to save her and take her with him into witness protection. Everyone was pleased after the interview was over. You know you'll have to come back and testify in open court Mr. Ortiz. Yes I do. I'm going to the Federal Prosecutor and see if we can go to the grand jury tomorrow and get a Rico indictment on our friend Soulja, said Agent Watts but I'm going to the judge now to get warrants to hit the crack houses and his personal house. The feds have been building a case against Soulja for about a year now and couldn't get enough to get an indictment but wit what Mr. Ortiz gave them and with his testimony they'll be able to put Soulja out what bank they would hit next and maybe they could catch them in the act. That would be lovely said Watts to himself.

(Business As Usual)

Since they put that new coke in the houses, business has been booming constantly. Lou can't sit down long before one of the houses is calling him to bring another 1000 count. Four days have passed since Soulja and .Special been on their bank heist and Lou has collected almost ninety grand from four houses. Lou missed Tye a lot because they were the closes of everyone in Soulja's crew. Soulja had money on the street for info on that snitch Simeon that set Tye up and Soulja said he had something for Detective Wilson for running him off the road like that. Everything Lou thought about that he wanted to mob into the Gary police department and gun det-Wilson down in front of everyone. As he drove through the streets in his Escalade Lou hoped things were going alright with Soulja and Special's mission. He talked to them earlier and found out that Soulja had been grazed and would be fine, but caught the news and saw they had gunned down a cop on their way out the bank. At least they got away thought Lou. Soulja had two days left and was still three hundred seventy five grand short of the million he needed. He Special and Tommy were in a slum hotel room outside of Minneapolis Minnesota where he planned to finish the last jobs then head back home. He talked to his daughters the other day and seen that they were okay but scared. He promised them he was coming to get them real soon and the phone hung up. Soulja talked to Sam earlier to and let him know how short he was and to find out if he got any more info on the Cubans. Sam found out the address of a couple of Carlos businesses in Miami and where a couple of his mini mansions were located because he flaunted his money and like to throw parties. Soulja said good look on the info, and they hung up. They ended the day by hitting two more local banks for a total of 165, 000. e way they were knocking the banks off they felt good about finishing up tomorrow as long as shit went as its been despite killing the cop everything has been sweet from them in and out. They flicked on the news and saw the broadcast of the several banks that have been robbed by two masked gunmen with semi-automatic weapons, and the report has the bulletin looking for two black males, because of the big clothes Special has been wearing and nothing about her actions have been girly. Soulja knows that banks are on their toes right now so he has to change it up for this last one, so he and Special talked about how hw wants this one done, then they drove back to Indiana to drop off the money they got from all the heist and to figure where the last 160, 000 gone come from. Tommy got a Malibu ready for tomorrows job parked and waiting. He tells them as they sit in the back room at Sam's. "Where did you park?" Said Sam, hoping he didn't park a stolen car in front of the club." It's down the block man, we cool," said Tommy. Sam went to check for himself while Soulja and Special counted the money." If you had seven hundred grand already why haven't you been bought this place," Said Special, knowing that Soulja had plans on buying Sam's club." Because I got to thinking bigger than Sam's and was trying to stack a little bit more because I want out the game Special, and now that Mesha dead I cant risk my freedom and my girls out here alone, you feel me," said Soulja. "Yeah but what you gone do about money cause once we pay this two mill, shit we back to square one in these streets, Said Special. "I'll figure something out," said Soulja. Then she knew he would to. "How many bricks we got left from Slick?" Asked Soulja. "About 30," said Special. " So we cool as far as dope goes?" Said Soulja. "Yeah we straight, but he didn't know that an indictment had just been handed down for him on Rico charges and a warrant for his arrest has just been issued and a ten man team are on there way with warrants as we speak to hit all the spots the informant gave them starting with the stash house." The survellience team said it's a one story brick house occupied by two female women and their home now." e house has cameras on each corner of the roof so we have to move fast said agent Watts over the radio. "Is everyone in place?" Unit one in place. Unit two in place, unit three in place.

(The walls fall down)

All unit sso was the call from Watts radio, and a four man team hit the front door after a two tap knockan call, (Police)!search warrant a team hit the back door and set up a 2 perimiter. Concussion grenades were sent in threw the side windows knocking the two women off guard. e cops put the women in cuff s, and cleared the house for anyone else but no one was there besides an ex-girlfriend of Soulja's name Jackie a thick chocolate beauty of Jamaican descent that he still knocks off and takes care of and her lil sister Tammy. Jackie is 28 and Tammy is 20.Soulja owns the house, but let's Jackie live there to keep up regular living appearance.

"House cleared," said one of the officer. "Are you sure there's drugs here?" Said an officer. Cause this place sure looks like to me a woman's pad with bra and panties all over shit in the back. "Yeah," said Watts going to a room used as the laundry with a washer and dryer. Informant said, "I would see a slide panel after I push this over." He pushes the washer over and see a slide panel by the floor. He slides the panel and there's 30 bricks of raw coke. They slap hands and smile. As Lou was leaving one of his girlfriends houses he fired up a blunt and turned his lil Wayne c.d. on. He was getting budded listening to fireman when an undercover got behind him and hit the lights for him to pull over. He seen them in time to toss the weed so he wondered if it was the eight grand worth of system that got him pulled over, it must be thought that Lou prepared to get a ticket for the sounds. He was strapped to, but he had all his papers, license, and insurance, so he wasn't gone let them search him or his ride. He was watching the two white boys on his back camera he had installed in the caddy truck. When he saw the words FBI on their shirts, they got out of the car and they both pulled their guns out ."Shit!" Said Lou to himself as he pulled his sig saver from under his driver seat and opened fire through his back window, hitting the passenger in his vest and knocking him down while the driver emptied his clip into Lou's truck as he sped off and hit a corner with the feds in tow, but Lou lost them after two quick turns, then he hit a alley and bailed out the caddy truck, and called for one of his girls to pick him up. The neighborhood was swarming with cops of all kinds looking for Lou's truck and when they found it he was nowhere to be found. He had jumped into Crystal's car and went to her crib so he could figure out what the hell was going on because that wasn't a traffic stop, they were coming to get his ass and he knew it.

He was named in the indictment but his warrant was only for questioning that's it but now he would have attempted murder charges on a federal officer .L.C was about to walk out the front door of the Delaney spot when he saw the under covers hitting the corner and he slammed the front door and yelled out cops and shot for the back door.

He made it out the back door right before the feds made it up the hill behind the house. They came up the block and from the next street over , but L.C made it out. His two workers got tackled in the back yard by cops.

They hit all of the dope houses that night arresting 9 of Soulja's guys, but they all followed the drill and the cops found not one rock or drug money out of none of the house. The only thing they found were the legal shotguns that were kept in all the spots.

The cops were pissed because they knew there was dope in these houses somewhere, but after searching for hours they concluded that they may have been waiting on the drop from the stash house they raided.

~ They took the 9 guys and gave them P.C charges to hold them for 72hours so the feds could see if they could get any of them to turn on Soulja. Soulja's house was also raided and they found two legal semi-automatics that were registered to Special and they found like six grand in Soulja's drawer, but the house was clean.

He had put the million 800 plus up in a spot only he and Special knew about, because he knew that if something happened to him that Special would still go and get his girls.

(Baby Girls)

Juan went by the stash house to check on his guest. He walked into the room they were in and told them that they would be going home tomorrow when there daddy would have his money.

"We wanna go home now." Said Marie crying on her sisters shoulder. "Well I'm sorry but you can't." Said Juan.

"Can we talk to our daddy?" Said Crystal.

"I let you talk to him already, but maybe later okay."

"Just stay quiet and eat your food." Said Juan.

He left then went into the other room that Tito was in, Pretty kids, I hope our friend meets his deadline said Juan.

"You're not really gonna kill the kids are you." Said Tito feeling for the kids.

"Of course not, said Juan you are, patting him on the back and walking out the door Juan called Soulja's phone." Hello said Soulja , I'll call you in the morning with the meeting spot, so please have all my money said Juan.

"You just make sure my girls stay healthy ."Said Soulja. "T hat's up to you my friend." Said Juan before hanging up.

(Bad News)

Lou kept trying Soulja's phone, but his Nextel kept going to voicemail. He talked to L.C and heard about the raid which made him call all the other houses but he get's no one. He knows something is up, so he calls some of the guys cribs and their girls all tell Lou their men are all locked up on P.C charges, and that the feds have them. Lou called Sam's and got no answer either. He tried Soulja, s phone again.

"Hello, said Soulja."

"Man I've been trying to get at you we need to talk, shit is real bad right now in the streets, I mean real bad. Soulja and Special were on their way to hopefully the last bank as they speak.

"I'm not in town right now but I'll get back at you in a few hours said Soulja".

"Look man don't go to old spots." Said Lou. "It's like that huh." Said Soulja.

"The big hats are knocking tough." Said Lou, meaning the feds have been threw.

"I got you bra." Said Soulja, not yet knowing the seriousness of what Lou was talking about. Lou text Soulja the chicks house number and told Soulja that when he got back into town to call his girl crib and not his cell phone.

"Be safe big bra." Said Lou.

"Fasho bra." Said Soulja hanging up then calling the lawyers office to see if he heard anything , but he wasn't there. So Soulja left him a message for him to call him A.S.A.P then he hung up.

"What's up said Special.

"I'm not sure yet," said Soulja. They were two blocks away from First National in Flint Michigan a nice sized bank that looked like it might have the last of what Juan wants for Soulja's kids.

(Damn)

Candy was chillin at home bored as hell so she grabbed her remote and started channel surfing then froze when she stumbled on a news report that involved a robbery that was at a bank in Flint Michigan and the robbers were still inside surrounded by thirty federal and local authorities. She was about to turn until she heard the reporter say that it isn't confirmed but one of the robbers is believed to be a man wanted by federal authorities named Ronnie Parelli, his accomplice is unknown at this time, said the anchor woman for channel seven news.

"Damn cuz what yo ass done got yoself into now, and she knew the accomplice was Special cause they were bread and butter. e bank was like two hours away from Candy so her mind got to working faster than normal. First thing she did was got on the phone and called Tammy. Tammy was one of Candy's soldiers, a 25 yr old 5 foot 11 medium build with a black belt karate, and with Candy's weapon training one bad bitch. Candy had a crew of 10 girls of which she trained on how to clean weapons and other arts of war she learned from her daddy, so now it was time to put shit in motion.

"Hey Tammy , said Candy threw her phone." "What's up Candy?"

"Wanna play?" I been waiting a long time for you to say that shit, hell yeah.

"Call the girls, and be ready in a half hour said Candy getting dressed. Candy had some new toys she had been wanting to try out anyway. She was thinking as she went into her basement and turned on the light.

Her basement, by first appearance looks like your regular neighborhood basement until she opens the door of her extra room with the tall mirror in front of the door. Once you move that and go into that room for millitants. Candy has all types of guns, smokers, infarred goggles, and AK's she was ready for war fasho. Most of the stuff was her pops, but she had got as good as he was with weapons.

Candy grabbed two duffle bags and started loading stuff in em. She didn't have a plan yet, but whatever she came up with she would be ready.

(Back to the beginning)

Special watched the feds snatch Tommy out the car and arrest him, then told Soulja. He knew he didn't give anyone a chance to hit an alarm then he thought about what Special just said, that the feds snatched Tommy out the car. is wasn't a button push, he knew it in his heart.

"What we gone do?" Said Special.

"Take the people and lock they ass in the back so they won't be in the way, because they not coming in as long as they know we got hostages." Said Soulja. Special took the ten to fifteen customers and locked them in a back room out of the way. is bank gave Soulja enough money pitting him at the two million he needed to get his girls back from Juan, but first he has to get out of this bank because jail wasn't an option at all.

Tomorrow was his deadline so he has to think fast.

"Ronnie Parelli, said one of the federal agents in charge over a bullhorn.

"Come on out the bank and give it up man, we got this place surrounded.

"How the fuck they know who in here , said Special waiting to here her name but never did.

"I don't know said Soulja thinking hard peeping out the bank windows.

"You think Tommy gave you up when they got him, said Special.

"Anything's possible, but the way this shit happened I don't think it's Tommy, said Soulja and it wasn't Tommy.

"Every since they snatched Tommy out the car and put him under arrest he hasn't said anything but his name. Specials phone rang and it was Candy. "What's up girl," she answered peeking out the window. "Look," said Candy, This is what I want yall to do." Meanwhile there was a female officer at one of The Blockades to keep traffic from entering the street. She turned around and noticed a woman crossing the street coming towards her car. Maam you need to go back the other way please, but the woman acted as if she didn't hear her command. "Excuse me?" She asked still approaching. "I Said You Cant Go This..." Was all she got out before the woman threw a chop to her throat which instantly disabled the officer, and dropped her to the ground. Candy rushed over with her duffel bag and helped Tammy put the cop in the back seat. She then pulled two remote controlled cars from her bag, setting the first one to the ground. She guided it down the street by the bank and to its final destination, under a cop car. She did the same with the second remote controlled car. Darkness had fallen, so the only way she was able to see her toys were by the ultraviolet lights she placed on the back of them. Other than that, they would've been lost. By that time, Tammy had done took the officers shirt and hat off, then sat in the drivers seat of her squad car. Candy crouched down on the passengers side handling business with a nice view of the bank, and the other cops who were half block away at the most. She got on her headset and called the other three girls. Candy asked if they were all in position and they all replied, Yes They Were. Soulja brought everyone from the back and placed them all by the front door just as Candy told him to. "I hope this shit work," said Special cocking her Gun. "What's the signal?" asked Soulja. She said, "We will all know it when it happens. As the swat team leader looked at his watch and told his men, Two Minutes We Go In, he was knocked down by the impact of an explosion. One of the police cars had blown up and before the cops could get themselves together, another car blew up killing six Federal officers and two detectives from the Flint Robbery Homicide Unit. As this was going on, the front doors of the bank opened and people started running in pairs of twos and threes in all separate directions. Snipers were reporting then someone on an empty rooftop began tossing smoke canisters into the streets. While the snipers took aim on the smoker; another sniper was taking aim on them. The first sniper caught a high power rifle cartridge to the chest knocking him back to his demise. The second cop sniper took one to the head making his head explode from impact. A third sniper realizing they were being picked off got down and radioed in that there was another sniper taking them out up there. The streets had so much smoke and madness, with people running in every direction, that no one noticed Soulja and Special jump in the car with Candy. They pulled off. Candy called her girls on her headset and made sure they were Ok which they were. That's what the fuck I'm talking about!" said Special, happy to be out that bank. "I bet ya ass will call me next time, wont you?" said Candy.

"Hopefully there won't be a next time." Soulja replied. "You think we can get the fuck out of this police car?"

"Fasho, cousin."

"Then I don't really care for riding around with dead cops in the back seat wit me." Soulja referred to the cop that Candy karate chopped.

"I feel you on that."

They pulled up to the other ride. Candy's other girls would meet up with her back in Indiana. She set the car on fire as they all jumped into the truck Candy drove in with Tammy. When they got back in their state, Soulja called Lou's girl's house and had the homie come to the hotel they rented. He spilled the whole events that went down with him and the other guys.

"Damn," Soulja said, not sure of his next move yet. First thing I gotta do is get my girls, then I'll deal wit this other shit. And plus, the lawyer hasn't called back yet. So, I still don't know shit. But I plan on staying low until I do. They said my name at the bank but I never took my mask off at none of them. So, they got an informant, but they can't prove it was me in there unless Tommy says he drove me there." He continued trying to make sense of it all.

"That's why you didn't answer the phone in the bank." Special put it together. "Cause yow knew they recorded that shit."

"Right." He confirmed.

"What the fuck happened!?" Director Johnson over at the Federal building screamed. "Could someone please tell me how a bank robbery turned into chaos like this? Ten officers are dead, and six are mine." His temper flared. "And the fucker got away from you during all this melee. Find this fucker! I don't care how you do it." Talking to his men. "Just find this fucker. Dismissed."

Juan called Soulja early that next morning and told him the exchange will happen in Miami because he didn't like Indiana. He advised Soulja to get on his way and call the number he gave him once he got there. Then he hung up on him.

Soulja had a quick meeting with the few people who were there. He told Candy to gather her crew and some real fire power to take to Miami with them. Also, he brought along Lou, L.C., Special, Tracy, and five other shooters who he kept on standby. Special asked if he was going to call Booby, but he declined. He had another mission for him. Then this phone rang and it was the lawyer.

"What's the word, man?" Soulja asked.

"Look, I won't beat around the bush with you. The FEDs have a warrant for your arrest; you were indicted under the Rico law. And, they've been raiding all your spots the informant gave them. And, he's agreed to testify for witness protection and immunity. He's giving them a hell of a circumstantial case, but with his testimony it will stick."

"Who's the informant?" Soulja needed to know.

"Well, it took me a lil' digging and a favor owed, but his name is Emmanuelle Ortiz."

"Emmanuelle Ortiz!" Repeated Soulja, shocked at the discovery.

"Sam!" Special added, just as dismayed because he knew about everything damn near.

"Yeah, he was arrested a few months back for trying to sell a kilo of cocaine to an undercover. And they found a gun with the serial numbers filed off. Consequently, they the life sentence shit at him or flip on you, and he flipped on you." Soulja was pissed off. He wanted to kill Sam badly because he trusted this mothafucker.

"Where is he?" Soulja asked.

"The FEDs moved him yesterday after they had him put a tracking device in a Malibu you were in, so they could know where you were."

"Son of a bitch." Was the only thing Soulja could think to say. "I'll get back to you."

"I'll see what else I can find out." The lawyer promised before they hung up.

"~ That's how they knew I was in the bank, and that's how they got there so quick. Nobody hit an alarm; that mothafucker Sam put a locater on the Malibu Tommy stole. Now I remember... when we were there counting the money he asked Tommy is he had that car parked in front of the club, and Tommy said no. But he still wanted to see. Ima find that mothafucker somehow, but let's get on the highway."

Miami

Soulja had the rims off his Hummer and the regular Hummer wheels put on. With it not so flashy, he could take it with him. - They had a total of twenty people-five trucks with one car that had a shit load of weapons with the driver inside.

He sent someone to one of the stash houses and realized it had been hit by the cops, which really hurt him because that was his get-back-on-stash. - They hit all his money machines and in one day the FEDs broke his baby empire down. Soulja was a thicker, and starting over was not an option. He and Special done been through too much to get where they were and now he got his snitch and this indictment. There was no way he could deal

with this shit broke, and plus he had his girls to take care of. Hell naw, he thought. Ain't no going backwards; something gotta give.

- They got to Miami that night. Soulja had someone to go get a room to lay low in while he called Juan and set up the meet. He used a pay phone because shit was too crazy right then to even think about using his cell.

"I see you made it." Juan told him the obvious. "Yeah, I'm here. Let's get this over with."

"Okay, one hour at this address." Soulja wrote down the info and Juan added,

"Don't fuck with me cause I'd hate to kill these beautiful little girls." Then he hung up.

FEDs

"What did you get from Ortiz?" Asked the director. 'Today was the day that Parelli was to have the money for his kids.'

"We've had Juan under surveillance for the past three days trying to see if he'd lead us to the kids. But so far, nothing."

"Our agents down there say that Juan is still there. So if they plan on meeting, it must be down there. So, get your team ready in twenty and take a chopper to Miami and get with the surveillance team." The director told Agent Watts. "It would be nice to get both Juan and this Parelli, wouldn't it?" He said to no one in particular. "Too many people have died in the past few days because of this Parelli. So, get to Miami and bring this son of a bitch in. Now, let's move."

Agent Watts got a six man team and headed to the launch pad with their bullet-proof gear. And their mini-14's. Ready for battle if it came to that.

Ever since Sam told the FEDs about Juan snatching Soulja's kids, they've had him under constant surveillance. - Their objective: to locate the girls. However, they had nothing but negative progress thus far.

"There's a two man team on Juan as we speak, so let's get there." Watts gave the order as they fled into the chopper.

E.P.A. around thirty-five or forty minutes." The pilot stated. "Okay. Let's move. "

Showtime

"Let's roll." Said Soulja, putting his twin Sig Sauers in his shoulder holster and grabbing the baby uzi off the seat. He cocked it. "Everybody know what to do?"

"Yeah." - They pulled off to meet

All Soulja had with him going in to get his daughters were Lou, Tracy, and one of Candy's girls named Crystal who was another dangerous bitch from Chicago, Illinois. She was 5'10" around 170; a red-bone from the projects who didn't give a fuck about shit and would smile at you right before she killed you. - They all were strapped real nicely and the rest of the crew had separate parts to play. Soulja had a headset on and they were situated close by if needed them.

Juan had Soulja meet him at a tow yard that they owned. When Soulja pulled in, he saw three Benzes and a Yukon parked out front. He didn't like the set up because they were on Juan's turf now. Soulja spoke into the headset before getting out of his truck.

"Special, what it look like?" She was looking through Candy's high powered infrared binoculars. Nothing seemed out of place.

"Everything looks cool. " She replied. "~ There's eleven guys and two kids in the truck by the heat signature."

"Keep ya eyes open." He told her.

"Out." Special turned to Candy, who was deep into the scope of her riffle. Ready to shoot somebody.

"Where do you get this shit?" Special asked about the infrared binoculars.

"Wouldn't you like to know."

"Fucking Ram-bitch." Special joked, then turned back around to watch Soulja as he got out the truck. Just as he did, the FEDs saw him and got on the radio to Watts.

"Okay Watts, It's going down at the tow yard right now. I have your man, Parelli getting out a white Hummer that's occupied by one Parelli is walking toward Juan who's standing in front if the Benz with ten men holding automatic weapons. Guys where are you?" Surveillance asked.

"We're five minutes from your location." Watts answered. "Just keep an eye on them."

"Ten-four." Picking up his binoculars and wishing he could get closer, which would only compromise their mission.

"Where's my money?" Juan inquired, not seeing any bags in Soulja's hands.

"Where's my daughters?" Soulja asked him a more important question.

Juan lifted his hand up and Tito let the girls out the truck. ~ They ran to their father. A sigh of relief had been let out.

"Once again, where's my money?"

Soulja made a hand gesture for Lou to bring two duff el bags over. ~ They were dropped on the ground right in front of Juan. Soulja kissed the girls and told them to go get in that truck. Once inside, Candy's girl got them out there like their daddy wanted her to.

"I don't have to count this, do I?" Juan began putting the money in his car "Where's your girlfriend? She promised me a dance."

"She couldn't make it."

"T hat's too bad." Juan commented while walking to his car, and before he got in it he told Soulja that it wasn't personal, just business.

73

Soulja got back in his Hummer. "Follow the money." Speaking into the headset to a trailer car that was sitting low waiting to follow Juan once he cut out from the tow yard.

"They're leaving," Stated the Fed surveillance. "Who do you want us to follow, Juan or Parelli?"

"I want Parelli." Watts told them. So, the agents followed Soulja's Hummer for four blocks until they lost tem in Miami traffic.

"Juan's team drove to Carlos' import/export warehouse."

"Okay Soulja, we got tem going into an import/export warehouse." I already know where you at from Sam's info. We're on our way."

"Go check things out for me, and let me know what were dealing wit." Soulja said.

"I got you. Special told him. She and Candy dressed in all black jump suits, looking like some sexy ass ninja's. They cut through the gate outside the warehouse with bolt cutters Candy had in her bag. Then they crept in to look around so they could get Intel before Soulja arrived. Once Soulja and the rest of the crew got there, Special and Candy had been in and out.

"Okay, said Candy, pointing at the nicely large warehouse." Up there pointing at some high up windows is an office and the rest is on the ground. They're in there putting boxes into trucks, and it looks like there may be close to twenty guys inside, and they're packing heavy."

"There's two in the top office." Special added.," And one looks to be Juan." "What's the plan?" Candy asked Soulja.

"Okay, split into three groups and enter from that side, that side, and the back.

And when you get my signal, you kill everybody that didn't come here with you." Soulja gave instructions.

"What's the signal?" Special asked.

"You'll know it. Now, everybody get to their places."

"Here's the money," Juan said, putting the duff el bags on the floor of Carlos' office.

"So, I see everything went good."

"Yeah, everything went as planned." Juan agreed.

"Good job, my friend. I knew you could handle this thing." Carlos told him. ~ They hugged. "Tell those fucking guys to hurry up loading those fucking trucks; I got two naked bitches in a Jacuzzi waiting for me."

"I got you, boss," Juan said, leaving out the office.

(Federally Ticked Off)

"What the fuck you mean you lost Parelli?" Watts said.

"Traffic got real thick and I'm sorry sir-we lost em."

"Well, where the fuck is Juan, cause somebody is going to jail tonight?"

"He went in the direction of that import/export warehouse they got. But, we don't

Have a warrant to go in there." The surveillance guy reasoned.

"Fuck a warrant." Watts jumped in the van with his team. "What's the address?"

(Ready Set Go)

Soulja sent three groups of four to wait on his signal and kept with him.

Special and Candy were together with Lou and one of Candy's girls, and Lana. They watched Juan come from upstairs hollering for the guys to hurry up so they could go. Then all you saw was the front slide-up door explode from Soulja's Hummer running through it and everyone of Juan's men opened fire on it.

And that was the cue for all hell to break loose. Everyone was firing off rounds.

As soon as his team started firing, Soulja and his five-man crew came out the bullet proof Hummer unloading shots at targets.

Juan pulled his Dessert Eagle out and took cover behind a truck, firing at Soulja's people. Carlos grabbed the uzzi he kept in his office and started raining down bullets on everything he saw from his office window, making everyone duck for cover.

One of Juan's men wasn't taking cover. He stood in the open shooting when he caught a slug through the chest. It knocked him into the truck he was standing by. Juan shot one of Candy's girls in the arm, knocking her to the floor.

Special and Candy were murdering everything in sight with their fully automatics. Candy spotted Carlos in the window on some Tony Montana, not afraid to die shit and took aim on him. She gave the boss a head shot that dropped him dead instantly. Juan watched Carlos fall and opened fire on Candy. The bullets barely missed her.

Soulja took out two of Juan's men as soon as he got out the truck. He was coming around one of the vehicles, but he didn't see Juan while Juan seen him and crept up on him. Special and Candy were on the other side of the warehouse and had a visual on Juan as he crept. The women both yelled for Soulja to look out, but they were too late because Juan was raising the Dessert Eagle as Soulja turned around.

Special dropped the empty assault weapon and pulled her nine out. She and Candy took off at the same time towards Soulja, raising their weapons to fire at Juan, but once Soulja turned, he saw that Juan had him cold. T en Juan fired, hitting Soulja in the chest knocking him backwards next to the truck. Special screamed Noooo as she and Candy came charging at Juan with a barrage of gunfire that riddled his body and dropped him to the ground. He still had some life in him when they made it over to him though.

"I told yo bitch ass we were gone dance, didn't I?" Special raised her gun and gave Juan a final head shot.

"They ran over to Soulja. She started to tear up because he wasn't moving, Special grabbed him.

"You can't die on me."

"I knew you were a pussy." He tapped on his chest to let her know he had on a vest. "Damn, that shit still hurt like hell."

"You had on a vest?" Special admitted to herself, glad about it.

"Yeah, after the cop grazed me at the bank, I wasn't sure how many more lives I had. So I got smart."

"Good thinking cousin." Said Candy.

"Everybody dead. Can we get the fuck outta here?" L.C came from Carlos' office with the two duffle bags in his hands. The money still in tact.

"Well, at least we ain't broke, "Soulja said. "Let's get out of here."

As everybody was getting ready to leave, something made Soulja check the boxes they were loading on the trucks. His eyes got big when he opened the first one that was being sent to Cuba. It was full of money, and the second, and in the third; there was like twenty five boxes piled up in the truck.

He checked the other trucks and it contained crates that came from Cuba. Soulja busted one of them open and found some art, but after he moved the straw around, he found ten keys of cocaine.

"Shit!" He said to Special. "You know if we take this shit, we gone have the cartel on our trails."

"Fuck em." She replied.

"Yeah., fuck em. Soulja agreed. He had L.C drive one of the trucks and he drove one. They would drive the trucks to the next city, rent a U-Haul to change up vehicles and put the shit in and dump the two trucks they had got.

In the rough gun battle, two of Candy's girls sustained minor injuries and Lou took one in the shoulder. One of Soulja's shooters got shot in the arm also, but no casualties.

"It's hot back home." Special noted. "Where we going?"

"Your name not hot." Soulja told her. "You can go home if you wanna."

"You think I'd leave yo ass like that; you crazy."

"Well, I got my girls, and it looks like we got money. So, we gone go wherever the wind blows us, but first, I got something personal to handle for Tye."

Lou get the info where that rat Simeon at who set up Tye."

"You know we gone see em, and I don't care how much money or time it takes, I'm gone find Sam, "Soulja vowed.

"Son of a bitch!" Agent Watts pulled into the warehouse and seen all the dead Cubans lying all over the place. "I guess our friend didn't take kindly to anyone taking his kids and making him pay for em, Huh?"
"Yeah.," Agent Young agreed. "It looks to me like he got his kids back and came and got his money back, And possibly more." Watts inspected all the

fresh oil spots and tire tracks that proved a truck had been there. "Get air support to fly in interstate and see if they locate two import/export cargo trucks. It's a long shot , but at this point it's all we got."

~The next day the two abandoned trucks were found in the next city over with no prints but Cubans on them.

"Well, whatever was in these had value, but what was it?" Watts wondered, looking through the back of one of the trucks. Get me a drug.

sniffer and let him walk the truck and see what he picks up." The dogs will bark, letting them know there were drugs inside."

(Never Forget Yours)

Soulja's haul turned out to be forty million dollars and a thousand keys of uncut dope. e nine of his partners would get out of jail after their P.C.'s the next day and not know what to do because they heard about Tye. Lou and Soulja was wanted by the FEDS, so the family was done. They heard the stash house got hit and all they got was the couple thousand in the drop boxes. So they didn't know what to do, but when they got home a few days later packages arrived that contained a hundred gees and two bricks, and a card that read:: For keeping it real and keeping ya mouth shut. One.

"What's up Special, what you reading?" Asked Soulja. "You remember Stacy, don't you?" Asked Special. "Yeah that nigga snitched on several cats in Gary to save his own rat ass in the federal system.

'What about him?" Asked Soulja.

"He out, and this his book." Said Special.

"I bet his rat ass ain't talking about all the tellin he did is he?" Asked Soulja, laughing out loud.

"Actually he's not to be honest, he lying to those who don't know him and he talking bout he was some kingpin of Gary." Said Special, .laughing out loud that's funny as hell there ."Before he turned into a rat for the feds he did use to get money in the dope game, but kingpin he needs to quit it ."Said Soulja, still laughing! "He better be watching his back, all the niggas he told on and got all that time may not appreciate his actions at all. "What you think?" Asked Soulja.

"Yeah, he deserves a bullet in that fat head of his for disrespecting the law of the game, meaning keep ya mouth shut , but he and a lot of other cats out of Gary done forgot that, I see, said Soulja.

"Yeah, the game done changed a lot, said Special.

"The game ain't changed babygirl just the players done got real weak, and it's gone take people like us to remind them of the rules. Feel me, like that fuckin rat bastard Simeon," said Soulja.

(Remember)

"Hello, this me, what up?" Said Soulja. One of his crooked connects heard about the hundred thousand dollar reward for Sam's where abouts. Soulja hired a bounty hunter he met at Sam's club one night. He and Sam were cool, but a hunnit grand tax free, fuck Sam he thought to himself the first time the job was offered to him.

Sam had a sister in Milwaukee that very few people knew about, not even Soulja new of her. He knew where his mom and dad lived, a few of his cousins, but the feds knew Soulja would go threw them to get to Sam so they all had been relocated into witness protection, except LoLo, Sam's oldest and most stubborn sister. Ms. Ortiz these people are killers, said agent Watts, and they won't hesitate to kill again to find your brother. I'm not leaving my house said LoLo.

"I've been living here for twenty years."

The scum in this city haven't chased me from my house and I don't plan on letting that scum chase me away either, and she meant it.

"We can't force you into witness protection Ms.Ortiz, but we have to inform you that your mom and other family members won't have any communication with you and you won't have any with them," Said agent Watts. That hurt LoLo because she was close with her family, especially her mom. LoLo's husband of ten years had been killed a few years back by a drunk driver while he was driving home from work. e guy was speeding when he ran a light, and rear ended Tony , LoLo's husband killing him instantly and destroying his car. e guy did two years in prison and LoLo got misery and heartbreak for life.

(Gotcha)

"Hello, mom is that you, said LoLo yes dear it's me, I thought you couldn't call me any more?

"It's been three months LoLo and I know it's your birthday so screw the FBI you're my daughter I love you and I miss you, said mom Ortiz.

"How is everyone mom?"

"Were okay. How are you LoLo?"

"I miss you, but I'm okay. Gotcha!" said the bounty hunter who was illegally tapping LoLo's phone and just found her mom who he was sure to be in arms reach of his payday Sam Ortiz. The bounty hunter found out Sam was in a quiet neighborhood in Oregon, waiting for Soulja to be arrested or hopefully killed then he won't have to testify. He hated the way things turned out, but he didn't want to go to prison for the drug sale. The bounty hunter had a friend at the phone company who he gave the number momma Ortiz was calling from and the friend gave him the address he was given by the bounty hunter then he hung up. Gotcha, thought Soulja .Ever since all the happenings of the previous days Soulja and Special been laying low tryna figure out there next move.

"Who was that?, Asked Special.

"That was the bounty hunter , he found Sam said Soulja.

"You want me to grab a few people and go murda that fuckin snake, said Special."

"Naw baby girl I want you to grab a couple of the guys and go get that bitch as nigga, and bring him back to me, I want to look him in the eye and let him know he hurt my feelings before I kill him," said Soulja.

"I'm on it boss," said Special, smiling because she knew Soulja was about to say something about the boss comment, she was right to. Cut that boss shit out girl, I ain't gone keep telling you that shit. She knew he had a lot of shit on his mind and she just wanted to comfort him and let him know she had his back, even though he knew that already.

(Lean Back)

Soulja was sitting back in recliner chair watching the news when Special walked up to the chair blocking his view of the tv letting him know she wanted all of his attention. She was dressed in a long t-shirt and panties.

"You know I was messing with you about that boss shit don't you, said Special?

"Yeah baby I know that.'

"You know I'm with you ride or die, said Special.

"From jump I knew you had my back if nobody else had it, said Soulja.

"So you know I love you and always have, said Special, taking hold of Soulja's hands.

"You're not about to ask me to marry you, said Soulja, making both of them break out laughing at the same time.

"Naw , boy I'm just saying, said Special.

"I know what you saying baby and I love you to, said Soulja pulling Special into the chair on top of him making her t-shirt rise up above that luscious ass of hers. Soulja stuck his tongue into Special's mouth as he pressed his lips to hers, rubbing down her back squeezing and gripping her ass still sucking on her lips. Soulja pulled her panties down her ass and halfway down her thighs. Special stood up and let her panties fall down to the floor, then took the t-shirt off as Soulja slid off his boxers he was watching tv in. Special took Soulja's dick in her hand and licked up the side of it before taking it deep into her mouth going up and down licking on the tip jagging him off as she went faster and faster .Soulja knew he had to stop her cause her warm mouth, soft lips, and the way she jacked his dick he knew he would come sooner than he wanted to, so he fought the sensation to let her keep going and pulled her into the chair.

She took his rock hard dick back in her hand and he gripped her fat ass spreading her ass cheeks as she guided his dick to her wet pussy sliding it deep inside of her, making her moan out as she went down with her ass, and he went up matching her thrust. Soulja licked and sucked on Special's nipples , taking his time as she rode his dick bouncing that fat ass taking him deeper and deeper. He played with her tits while licking her nipples driving her crazy. She wrapped her arms around his neck, as he reached back down grabbing and gripping her ass speeding her pace. They both felt their climax close to being reached, and with a final push and thrust from each other they both climaxed at the same time even tho Special had cum two other times during the thrusting , but that last one was the best one she thought to herself.

"Now I need a shower, said a tired and sweaty Soulja. "I'll meet you there, said tired still horny ass Special.

(Road Trip)

The next day Special, Lou, L.C, and two of L.C's lil niggas went on a road trip to Oregon to see an old friend. Agent Watts came by the Ortiz house to check on their status and to let them know that they still haven't located Soulja yet.

"We will locate him, said agent Watts, and until then I still ask that you don't contact any old friends or family that didn't come into witness protection with you and your family that's here in Oregon now. Sam his mom and another sister were staying together and other members of the family were in other houses of the city.

"We understand, said Sam to agent Ortiz . "I'm sorry Mr. Watts, said mom Ortiz. "Sorry for what Ms. Ortiz, said agent Watts.

"My daughter LoLo birthday was the other day and I had to talk to her, we are all she has since her husband was killed.

"Oh, mom, said Sam.

Red flags went off in agent Watts head as he grabbed his cell phone rushing to call the Oregon field office .

"This is agent Watts. We may be compromised. Send me an abstraction team to this location ASAP." Then he hung up the phone, drew his nine millimeter from his shoulder holster.

"Get your things together a team will be here in a half hour to take you some place else, this location may have been compromised," said agent Watts to the Ortiz family. He peeked out the blinds into the dark night and checked his clock hoping his team made it before any unwanted guest arrived. Watts told his partner on the porch out front what was going on and to be on alert until the abstraction team made it there in about 30 minutes.

"My mom said she only called that one time and she swears she didn't tell LoLo where we are, said Sam to agent Watts.

"We can't take any chances Mr. Ortiz you're to valuable to this case, and I'm sure Parelli knows that, just like we do, that's why we have to move you again. The abstraction team churped Watts from around the corner letting him know they will be there in 30 seconds.

(Times Up)

"Let's go, said Watts, to the Ortiz family, my team is around the corner. ~ ey followed Watts out the front door and towards the street. He saw his team pulling up the street in two dark surburbans as they reached the curve and as they were pulling up he looked the opposite direction and saw a Ford 150 being trailed by a tinted out excursion truck, then Watts felt like he was in a movie cause everything got quiet and went into slow motion. Before he could signal his team or get the Ortiz family back into the house, the doors on both the f150 and the Excursion were popping open and the same went for the abstraction team doors then all hell broke loose in the streets. Special was the first one to hit the streets in all black with her mask and vest, firing into the lead abstraction team truck with her chrome trimmed AK47 fully automatic with a hunnit round drum killing the driver instantly with a head shot. e rest of the team hit the ground unable to return fire. Watts made the Ortiz family hit the ground until he could get them to safety. He returned fire at the assailants .The rest of Specials team, vest, powerful armor, piercing weapons and mask evacuated their vehicles firing wildly at the abstraction team as well as Watts and his partner who were firing back every chance they got. The best Watts could do for Sam and his family was hide them behind the riddled Surburban truck that his team had jumped out of and were firing assault rounds back at the hit men. "This is agent Watts of the FBI to anyone listening we need immediate assistance." Watts yelled into his radio on an open police frequency so that all available agencies near by heard the call and they did. County police, city cops, Feds were all tryna get to their brothers assistance. It was like the fourth of July out there flying everywhere, glass breaking from near by houses and every vehicle in the area. People were ducking to the floors all around from the close sounds of shooting and some from bullets entering their houses threw windows and walls. L.C and his guys shot it out with the abstraction team while Special and Lou crept up on Watts position. A team member tried to change position from behind a tree to a better line of sight to ire from, but was hit in his vest by two rounds from L.C's weapon and the rounds pierced threw his vest and heart blowing him back into a tree then to his death.

Agent Watts opened fire wildly at the enemy after seeing another agent fall. One of L.C's guys were hit in the neck from return fire making him drop his gun and grab his neck giving the feds an opening and one took it shooting the soldier in the head killing him instantly. Special and Lou flanked Watts and came up from behind creeping through the neighbors yard. Watts and his partner were busy firing at the hit crew when they noticed they weren't being fired at anymore, at that moment Watts heart skipped a beat as he spun around just as Special and Lou had crept up on them. Watts raised his pistol squeezing off a barrage of bullets at the figures hitting Special in the vest, making her lose her balance, but still standing, then Lou riddled Watts with bullets starting at his chest to his head. He lived for about 5 seconds. His partner noticing Special didn't fall from the chest shot, knew they had vest on. He screamed Watts name as he saw him fall to the ground dead, he opened fire on Lou , hitting him dead center forehead dropping him Just as Special was regaining her composer. She wanted to cry seeing Lou fall, but was so mad at the moment she just held the trigger on her fully AK47 an shot Watts partner about twenty times each armor piercing round going through the officer and the truck behind him even killing Sam's mom. All the shooting left Sam alone cowarding on the ground behind the truck with a bullet in his arm. To anyone else you would have thought Special was a dude in the loose fitting all black and ski mask, but Sam new who she was. Special don't kill me, I know that's you please, I wasn't gonna testify, I just said I would so I wouldn't go to jail for the dope I was caught with, please Special.

"Look around you fuckin rat, said Special. There are people dead and on the run because of yo bitch ass running your mouth. Special pointed the AK at Sam, Special please you can come with me they will move us anywhere we wanna go please Special. Special let the AK down and Sam exhaled.

"We will be together one day Sam, said Special raising the AK back up. I'll see you in hell mothafucka," said Special squeezing off the remainder of her drum into Sam's body.

She had zoned out and was empty but still squeezing the AK trigger until L.C ran to her and broke her zone she was in cause he heard cop sirens very close. Everyone was dead that came with Special but L.C, plus all the feds were dead in what would go down as one of the most deadliest shootouts with the cops in history leaving 10 federal agents dead, four masked hit men, a federal witness, his mom and sister, plus property damage in the hundred thousands. The investigators would find over two hundred shell casings at the grizzly crime scene. Special looked at Lou and the other fallen soldiers as they ran to the truck and sped off only to swap it out before hitting the highway.

(FEDS)

The director got the call and almost blew a blood vessel when he heard about the witness and his men, the only relief he got was hearing about the dead gunmen, but was angry again after getting witness reports of a couple more shooters that fled the area in a stolen truck that was located a few blocks away burning, and the shooters were no where to be found. ey had on mask so the witnesses couldn't describe them to a sketch artist. He knew they were Soulja's men but couldn't place Soulja at any crime scene and with the death of Sam he may have lost his federal case against Soulja, but after seeing his men dead like that he had no intention on letting Soulja make it to a court room alive.

(Now What)

"You know you can go home Special, you don't have any warrants on you, and the attorney said your name came up but that's it," said Soulja.

"Sam's bitch ass dead, you can go home now to, said Special.

85

"Naw babygirl not yet, shits been hectic, cops been killed , my people been killed and they know they may can't prove I was there or had it did , but they know I had something to do with it so I have to do it right. The attorney said stay low for a while," said Soulja.

"Well I'm with you all the way," said Special. Soulja smiled and tossed Special a envelope.

"I knew you would say that. She opened the envelopes and inside were new id's, socials, birth certificates, and credit cards for her and Soulja.

"That's what's up," said Special looking at the I.D for her.

"Nice pic," said Special smiling to herself , so where we going .

"Have you ever been to Amersterdam," said Soulja smiling to Special.

"Hell naw, but should I pack phillys or backwoods," said Special smiling back because she knows that the weed and weed laws were different there and she was with it.

"I got it all under control, said Soulja." Get your stuff together we got a plane to catch that takes off in 60 minutes from now. Even though it was a private plane Soulja purchased from the drug money they took from the cartel, so they had as much time as they wanted. The plane wasn't going anywhere til Soulja said so.

(L.C)

L.C got five million dollars for his part in everything that went down, like helping get Soulja's girls back and going to is it Sam, but mainly for being real to Soulja from day one and never going astray. L.C didn't have warrants so he went home back to Gary, Indiana where he was born and raised. He was trying to talk his mom into moving out of the city with him cause they had money now, but she said she was home and didn't want to leave her city. After fighting with her for a few days she allowed him to buy her a house in the deep Glen Park area of the city where the crime is lowest, and the houses are the nicest. He bought her a beautiful two story brick house that had three bedrooms, two bathrooms, a patio, fireplace, full basement, and a two car garage. He told her that she could walk into the house from the garage.

"What am I gonna do with a two car garage L.C, said his mom." I only got one car pointing her ten year old Chevy truck.

"I don't know ma hitting the garage button making it rise up revealing a spanking brand new six hundred Benz all white with leather black interior. Everything factory because he didn't want no one tryna carjack his mom for no damn rims. L.C's mother loved him to death and knew he more than likely did wrong to get his money, still she never questioned him , partly because she didn't want to know, and partly she knew he wouldn't stop even if she ask him to, cause his and her life was hard coming up without his dad. Mom did what she could to raise her son, and he knew his mom loved him. She loved everything he bought her, all she had to do was go in the house he had it fully furnished with top of the line furniture, big screen plasma TV's, alarm systems for the house and the car. Mom was straight and he sealed it with a kiss.

"Here you go ma, passing his mom a platinum card with unlimited credit. She teared up hugging her son telling him to be careful. She prays for him every night and she loves him.

"I love you to ma, said L.C.

Soulja had plugged L.C with the right people to legitimize his money with the right investment. L.C purchased golden aces a night club on Chicago's Southside, and on this night he was interviewing two of the girls inside his spanking new platinum color 760 BMW on all chrome twenty three inch rims with the heated loui seats, three tv's, sunroof plus a sound system that would make you rather walk home than ride in this car. Listening to 2-pacs Dear Mama. Tonight he was rolling at half max, and it sounded like it was at max, but who cared cause it sounded good. ~ e one in the back seat name was Shay-Shay a 23 yr old brown skinned five five, 150 lbs, shoulder length hair Jamacain and Hatian dime with a tiny waist line, Stacy Dash face, Halle Berry tits, Vida Guerra ass, and a pair of Carmellita legs and thighs. e one up front name was rain, a 25 yr old 130lb red bone with Jada Pinkett face and body,

~These were two cold women that L.C stole out of Florida strip club and brought them back up North. If it wasn't for the limo tint on the windows of the BMW, anybody they rode by would be able to see the freshly shaved pussy of rain protruding out from under the very small mini skirt as she gave L.C head, and the deeper she took him into her throat the higher her ass and skirt rose up for the world to see if they could. He reclined his seat and used his free hand to reach into the backseat and finger Shay-Shay, as she played with her own nipples. L.C knew he would have to have his seats cleaned in the morning but forget it now he got money he thought. Shay-Shay turned around putting her knees on the seats, spreading her legs wide dropping her ass into L.C's hand and he played with her pussy, while she moaned and looked out the back window. They had hit several blocks and made several turns.

(Americas Most Wanted)

"My name is Josh Walsh and this is America's most wanted and tonight the Indiana field offi ce of the FBI needs your help to catch a ruthless and very dangerous criminal name Ronnie Parelli. Agents say Parelli may be behind the deaths of several U.S Marshalls, police officers, state witnesses and more.

"Agents say they need your help in locating Parelli cause right now he could be anywhere.

"Parelli is six foot 2 190-200 lbs he has tattoos on his chest, back, both arms, and forearms. He keeps his head bald."

"Parelli is to be considered armed and extremely dangerous so don't try to apprehend , just call our tip line at 1800-AMW-9457 your name will remain anonymous." Members of the fugitive task force watched the tv as John Walsh asked the public for help in finding Soulja cause the marshals couldn't is what John Walsh should have said.

"I hope this works, said the agent in charge because I really want this mutherfucker bad. Around ten agents sat in silence watching the large screen show Soulja's face to the world and to let them no he was a monster and enemy to every state let them tell it.

"Gotcha!" You son of a bitch, said an agent named Jones to the screen. Jones was a thirty year old ex Dallas Homicide Detective who had some strings pulled by a uncle in Washington who got him into the FBI after only being a cop for five years. He was out to prove himself and Parelli would be the one he said to himself.

(Stuff ain't sweet)

Who is that following us, was all Shay-Shay got to say before the HK bullet shattered the back window of L.C's BMW then ripping through her forehead killing her instantly then lying to rest in the back of her brain. T e impact from the blast knocked Shay-Shay back and into the seats then to the floor.

"Shit, said L.C as he jerked the wheel and pushed Rain off who had a mouth full of manhood. He leaned to the glove compartment and grabbed his all black glock 45 while Rain balled her tiny frame up on the floor screaming and crying. He wanted to put her ass out cause she was distracting and irritating him right now when people were tryna murda him, but who he thought. The two Columbian hitters had been following L.C. for a while and were waiting for him to stop to get him, but he just kept on riding, so when they saw Shay-Shay looking out the back window they felt she saw them, so they changed plans and opened fire. They wanted the reward from the cartel for the heads of Soulja and his tops and when they say heads they meant chop the heads from the alive or dead body and bring it to them. L.C fired out the shattered back window at his attackers tryna get them off his trail. He noticed they were in an older model car and hoped his new BMW could out run the older car, but the super charged big block up under the hood of the Chevy nova wouldn't be bullied by the speed of the newer car. Bullets riddled the back lights and the trunk of the BMWQ as they shot it out threw traffic in the busy Chicago streets.

L.C squeezed off round after round at the nova and driving at speeds close to 90 weaving in and out of traffic.

"Shut the hell up and get me a clip out the glove compartment if you wanna live, said L.C. to Rain. At first she wouldn't move but she didn't wanna die so she grabbed another clip and stuck it in the 45 for L.C.

"Stay low and be quiet said L.C to Rain.

"I'm tired of this shit. L.C saw that he was headed for a big intersection get me another clip out the glove compartment, hurry, said L.C to Rain. She gave him the clip , he sat it between his legs and told her to hold on as he hit on his breaks making the shooters ram into the back of the BMW throwing both driver and shooter off balance. The shooters head hit the dash board making him drop his gun. The driver regrouped faster and took back off after L.C .T at gave L.C enough space to speed up and spin his car sideways as if blocking the street.

The Columbians sped toward L.C and as the shooter was regaining his composer getting ready to fire L.C opened up out the drivers window aiming with two hands and closing one eye. He emptied every bullet into the nova hitting the passenger center chest with a three round burst and the rest went through the car and some into the radiator, but the driver was still flying towards L.C intent on killing him with his car since his buddy was dead. L.C switched his clip in a motion move the average person wouldn't have believed it was that fast. Then he opened back up on the nova. hit him. A round caught the driver in the shoulder tearing threw his rotor cup then another hitting him high chest making him swerve and crash into a pole. L.C knew he needed to go before the cops came but he ha dto know who were tryna kill him. So he jumped out the use to be beautiful BMW telling Rain to stay in the car, 45 in hand approaching the riddled and smashed up nova. He expected to see black guys who if were alive would say some shit about some old beef or what ever, but he was shocked to see Columbians.

"What the fuck?" Said L.C, to the barely alive driver.

"Who sent you at me pussy?' Said L.C smacking the driver in the head with his 45 cause he knew the cops were close so he had to hurry. e driver smiled and revealing blood red teeth.

'Fuck you, was all he said to L.C. So he raised his 45 shooting the driver high in his opposite shoulder.

"Who sent you , said L.C.~ e cartel wants you and your friends dead for stealing from them and even if you kill me there will be more coming motherfucker said the Columbian smiling again in pain.

"Oh yeah, thanks for the info said L.C shooting the driver in the head twice .Rain wanted to run but her legs wasn't working .L.C knew he should kill Rain now cause she knew and saw to much, but he couldn't do it for some reason. He hoped he didn't make a bad decision.

"Sorry about your friend said L.C looking back at the dead body in his backseat as he hurried to get out the area cause he had to dump the body and figure out what to do with Rain.

"You're not gonna kill me are you, said Rain.

"I thought about it for a minute, said L.C meaning every word of it. As a as she concerned she wasn't my friend , she was just another bitch taking money out my pocket, meaning she was the competition, said Rain.

"I just met her at the club. LC one again used one of Soulja's plugs, and twenty five grand later Shay-Shay's body would never be seen again and a rumor would get started that she went to New York.

"What am I suppose to do with you said L.C to a calmer Rain. L.C had one of his people bring him a ride to switch out the BMW. They brought him his white on white caddy escalade on twenty four inch flats, with all competition speakers, amps, and radio. Rain loved the BMW, and now the caddy truck, she knew he was paid.

"Take me with you," said Rain. .L.C figured since he almost got her killed that he owed her tonight and probably a lil paper to, he thought.

(Life's Good)

It was like 85 close to 90 degrees outside as Candy and three of her girls rode threw Atlanta's Westside in her brand new Lexus convertible on twenty inch Ashanti rims, candy apple red with the white guts, kit and all. They were styling for sure turning heads every corner they turned and if the car jackers that saw the Indiana plates on the Lexus full of women would have known it was Candy and her crew was then maybe they wouldn't be following Candy's car now. Soulja gave Candy 5 million dollars two of which she hooked her girls up so they down in the ATL checking on some property Candy purchased, like her beauty parlor, and an ice cream shop. She said she always wanted all you can eat ice cream.

The beauty parlor was in the center of a very packed strip mall and all eyes were on the convertible Lexus banging Ushers, You got it bad. Candy pulled in front of her shop and when she stepped out the car , all you saw first was some of the sexiest legs coming from up under a Versaci skirt with the matching top that showed off her belly ring and her perky tits. Her designer shades matched her designer shoes, Candy was killin 'em right now and she had three bad dangerous bitches with her. is day she had Brenda a 26 year old dark skinned 165 pounder that stood five seven. She had a body like Mrs. Parker off Friday for real and this day she may have had her blue shorts on cause that's all you saw when Brenda stepped out the passenger seat. She had to pull them out her but because they rose up during the ride. Then there was Vicky a 25 year old peanut butter color stallion that stood like five ten or eleven depending on her shoe choice for the day. She was a solid 170lbs with a fl at stomach, handful of breast and a ass you could rest on after a real workout. She was in a baby fat hookup all pink from the hat to the glasses, top to the tight bottoms that kept the babyfat words on her ass, bouncing like crazy ending at the shoes. And finally there was twin a 21 year old baby face white girl. She was five two and weighed a good 120lbs. She ran track in school and stayed toned up. Her stomach and calves were on point and she had a very nice tight ass that stood up perfectly in her Gucci designer outfit and sunglasses.

"Them some bad bitches, said Rayvon from the passenger seat of the stolen jeep Cherokee parked across the street watching Candy and the girls get out the Lexus.

"Yeah, I know , but fuck them hoes." We gone get paid off that Lexus bro, said Maine from the drivers seat. Maine and Rayvon 2ex burglars and car thieves turned carjackers met in the juvenile center when they were kids. Now ten years and two prison bids later they are still at it, except they up the anty to car jacking. Just looking at these chicks Maine knew there was something about them that was different than other women they had staked out. Maybe it was how cold some of their looks were, or how they seem to stay aware of their surroundings, naw he was just tripping he thought to himself these just some fine ass dope boy hoes from out of town that are about to be jacked thought Maine. Maybe he should have paid more attention to how all of them carried their handbags, so close to them.

"It's about to get dark, said Maine, we got 'em soon as they come out that shop because all the other places are starting to close up now.

"This is nice, said Brenda to Candy complementing the shop. Candy had spent some real money on her shop, she put big screen t.v.'s an her waiting area, video games, plus a day care for the little kids and all the best equipment you could buy.

"Yeah the grand opening is in two days said Candy.

"Girl let's go get something to eat, I'm hungry said Vicky.

'Bitch yo ass always hungry, that's why ya booty looks like Buffy's now cause you eat so damn much, said Candy, making all the girls laugh out loud.

"Naw bitch this ass fat like this from Brenda's daddy hittin it from the back, said Vicky getting down on all fours shaking her butt at her friends. They all laughed again.

"You nasty as hell, said Brenda knowing Vicky had a crush on her dad, but knew she was just playing.

"Let's roll yall, said Candy. The girls exited the shop, walked towards the Lexus out front and as soon as Candy hit the alarm button on her car the stolen jeep was pulling up behind them blocking the car from being able to pull off.

"What's up with yall, said Rayvon to Candy from the passenger seat.

"Can me and my guy get down with yall?" Brenda and twin went around to the passenger side like they were about to get in that side but they were on point as Candy was to.

"Naw boo I don't think my lady would like that, said Candy smacking Vicky on the ass making her jump a little bit.

"So can you please move your truck so I could pull out, said Candy to Maine as she was about to open her door Vicky stepped behind her and at the same instance both doors on the jeep popped open and the driver and passenger jumped out, guns drawn expecting an easy lick.

"Bitch you should have let us get down with yall, now we want your car," said Rayvon, raising his gun towards Candy but noticing she didn't have a inch of fear in her eyes.

"Fuck yall," said Candy as twin came from behind Candy with her all chrome 380 automatic catching Rayvon off guard squeezing the trigger in rapid motion hitting Rayvon four times in the chest knocking him into the jeep, then to the ground making him drop his gun, then grasp for air as his lungs filled with blood making him drown and die in minutes.

Before Maine made it around the jeep to aid his fallen friend Brenda and twin had already had the ups on him. Twin fired through the open passenger window from the passengers side of Candy's Lexus hitting Maine threw the shoulder through the jeeps front windshield knocking him off balance but not down. He tried to raise his weapon to fire but Brenda was ready and caught him with a two squeeze motion from her glock nine millimeter dropping Maine by piercing his heart and killing him instantly. Candy was armed to, but she had total faith in her girls, plus she knew they had to involve the cops on this one and she was the only one that didn't have a gun permit.

"Welcome to ATL bitch," said Brenda to Candy.

"Yeah, I know," said Candy.

"You didn't have to smack my ass that hard bitch," said Vicky rubbing her butt, that shit hurted.

"No more carjacking for those fuckers," said twin putting her gun back in her bag.

"Can we go get something to eat now said Vicky." I'm still hungry. They all stood there laughing and unphased from the nights event.

"Now we gotta deal with the damn cops," said Brenda.

"Yeah, said Candy yall no what to do. Twin started talking in a shiver like she was scared to death, then started laughing.

"Yeah we know what's up. By the time the cops left , they figured it self defense by the sexy out of town girls who had gun permits and were shaking and crying when they arrived, plus they knew Rayvon and Maine were known carjackers they were looking for at the time of their murders.

"Let's eat ladies, said Candy putting in her Nikki Minaj CD turning up the volume as they rolled out the parking lot.

(Decisions Decisions)

L.C hit the highway and went to his crib in the suburbs of Chicago where all of the goody goodys stayed. It was a plushed out five bedroom, three bathrooms with a real fire place in the master bed room, three car garage where he kept his six hundred Benz, his phantom and the BMW that got shot up earlier. His house had a pool, a patio, big screen plasmas all over. Rain had completely calmed down and talked herself into believing L.C wasn't going to kill her. She felt like she was on cribs or at a rappers crib and she didn't want to leave. They both had blood on their clothes so L. C gave Rain a tee shirt and towel and showed her to the shower and told her to give him her clothes, She stood there in front of him and stripped down naked to her thongs and matching red bra. She gave him her clothes then asked him did he want these too, tugging at her thongs smiling at him. Naw ma you can keep them said L.C. taking her clothes over to the fire place and tossing them in and watching them burn, then he stripped down and did the same with his clothes. Rain was in his shower washing off any traces of the night when L.C. came into the shower taking the soap out of her hand standing behind her, he started lathering her blackened arms. She placed her arms against the shower wall and spreaded her legs like the cops were about to pat her down. L.C. went down rolling the soap over her ass and then between her cheeks going deeper til his hand was rubbing the soap over her soaking wet pussy making her moan from the touch. He turned her around and did the same to the front taking his time at her nipples making them swell up as he played with each one as he soaped them up, she was on fire. My turn said Rain taking, taking the soap from him and lathering his chest and arms then dropping down on her knees lathering his legs and thighs going up to his balls, then lathering his man hood with both hands jacking him to erection. Rain took him into her mouth as the warm water sprayed both of them from the shower head. She took him deep into her mouth slowly then released to the tip licking him and sucking him all the jacking him off. Then she speeded up her pace taking him deeper into her mouth making her gag as she bobbed back and forth jacking him all the time. He knew if he let her go any longer he would cum sooner than he wanted to. He reached to his shower shelf outside the door and grabbed a condom he brung into the bathroom with him and put it on turning her around bending her against the wall he entered her super wet spot from the back, holding her hips he stroked her hitting her spot with every stroke making her scream out in exstacy.

"Damn L.C baby don't stop ooh shit don't stop damn baby said Rain, making L.C hit it even harder making her cum several times from that position. He then turned her around picking her up and sliding her down on top of him holding her by the ass against the wall digging into her as she held him around the neck thrusting her hips as she rides him faster and faster going harder and harder into her until they both came damn near dropping to the floor.. They showered and dried off then went into L.C's master bedroom.

"Now what, said Rain? Looks like you got the job," said L.C smiling at Rain tossing her an envelope with cash in it.

"What's this for, said Rain?

The envelope had twenty thousand dollars in it and it was for Rain's silence and for her to say that her girl left town after changing her mind about working here. L.C believed it was easier to use her then kill her. He hoped he was right and plus he liked shorty.

(Amsterdam)

Everything went just as planned, paperwork, the flight now we here, said Soulja to Special as they stepped off the jet to a waiting hummer limo.

"Damn I can get use to this said Special.

"You ain't seen nothing yet babygirl, said Soulja, pouring Special a glass of dom p. from the bar in the back of the limo. The limo pulled up in front of a mini mansion gated away from the neighbors with a pool and hot tub outside in the back of the crib. Special never saw so much land.. "Who gone cut all that damn grass," said Special.

"You will look hot in booty shorts, a sports bra riding on a driving lawn mower said Soulja laughing.

"I bet I would," said Special punching him in the arm. e inside was plushed fasho, six bedrooms, four bathrooms, two dining rooms, a huge living room, furniture shipped from Europe, everything brand new like Soulja asked for. He had a crooked contractor and real estate agent that plugged him under the table with paperwork and furniture for a small fee of a hundred grand a piece for their time. Soulja dropped six and a half million for the crib.

"Let's roll, I wanna show you something else before we lean all the way back from that long flight. They jumped back into the hummer hitting traffic pulling in front of a huge strip club called club A.I.T.

"I know you didn't," said a smiling Special as they got out of the limo walking into the front door of the club that was three times the size of Sam's club.

"Damn, said Special, as they entered the booming strip club that was packed at 7pm on a Tuesday. E club had forty of the if nest women of all colors and sizes from small and petite, to thick and damn thick. Over the bar was a big screen TV that showed paper view fights and sport events. Ree stages jumped at the same time with women pussy poppin on a hand stand. The best d.j in town playin the music which blared out of every corner in the club. Soulja's office had a big screen TV that he could by remote switch to the private rooms to make sure the girls were safe and doing only what their suppose to do. He had a couch, wet bar and a huge vault behind the wall. E contractor hooked him up with the club.

"This what's up," said Special. Soulja's phone rung he wrote something down then hung up.

"I found that rat Simeon," said Soulja Call and handle that or let me go back and take care of it," said Special.

"Naw baby I owe Tye this one, ima handle this one myself, but I want you to stay here and chill and as soon as this bitch is dead I'm right back you feel me. Special didn't want him to go without her or even let him go period, but she knew when his mind was set and plus it was personal after the snitch set up Tye and got him killed., so she just said ok and leaned back. Soulja called L.C and told him what's up and where to meet him at what time and what to bring.

"Be careful said Special don't make me have to come back and murder a muther fucker cause something happened to yo ass said Special. And he knew she meant it.

"I will baby girl I'm in and out you feel me. I'm to hot right now to be bullshitting around, but I have to handle this you feel me, said Soulja.

"I feel you," said Special. Soulja called and told them to have the jet ready to roll in one hour, he was on his way. When he got to Chicago L.C was waiting for him in the caddy truck.

"What's up my nigga?" Said Soulja.

'It's all good," said L.C. They hadn't talked since the night the guys tried to kill L.C, he let Soulja know the cartel had hits on them.

"You being safe," said Soulja to L.C," after the near death experience?

"I'm good now," said L.C, knocking on his fresh bullet proof glass he had installed in his truck.

(Awww Rats)

As Simeon was walking into his crib from leaving the Narcotics department to give them other names he knew of guys who were dealing, he kept saying better them than him because he was a known coward and couldn't do prison time. He was pulled over one night after running a light with two ounces of crack cocaine in the car. This nigga got to talking as soon as the cops found the dope. So, he'd been snitching to the cops for the last few years. This girl hooked him up with big Tye. That's how he set him up, but that case was closed after Tye was killed from the crash.

Soon as he closed the door to his apartment, he was hit hard in the head with the butt of L.C's Dessert Eagle. The blow knocked him unconscious. When he awoke his head was killing him; his hands and legs were tied and he was naked. Plus, he felt like he'd been stung by bees all over his body.

He realized he was in a box of some sort. Soulja walked up to the box and Simeon knew who he was. He knew that Tye was his boy, therefore, he knew he was a dead man. Soulja had no intentions of listening to this coward cry for his life, so he gagged his mouth.

"Listen up closely." Soulja told him." As you know, you fucking rat bastard." You are about to die." He continued looking down on the snitch." I know you know that, don't you?" And you're praying it goes quick, and I'm happy to tell yo bitch ass that it won't." As you see, you're naked, and I'm sure your body stings all over." Pausing to let the victim absorb what he was saying amongst the pain he felt." Well, that's the fifty or so paper cuts you say."

Just then L.C poured a box of like twenty big ass rats on top of Simeon. ~ en Soulja had a top threw over him right before they dropped the box in an open grave at the Oak Hill Cemetery in Glen Park. Simeon helplessly screamed and tried to fight off the rats, but his mouth was covered, and his hands and feet were tied. Eventually, he prayed that he suffocated before the rats ate him up.

"Oh-yeah." Soulja said before they filled the hole with dirt." Just in case you're hoping to suffocate, I had a hose put in too, just to make sure that you and your friends are breathing fine." He would survive for hours with the hungry rat's eating on his flesh, piece by piece, killing hi slowly. His last moments were spent wishing he could have been a man and stood strong, but now, he would die a coward and nobody would even know where he was.

"Bye you fuckin rat!" L.C added as he started piling dirt onto the grave that now was Simeon Bradley.

"What now?" L.C asked Soulja. "You can't go back home."

"Well bra, you can, and that means you gone hold things down here until I figure things out." Soulja answered." I can't run forever with my girls, man. But, I can't take care of the fro prison either, feel me, pausing in momentary thought. My main thing is I gotta lay low, but for how long, I don't know yet.

Special doesn't have any warrants; I told her to stay here but she refuses to leave my side."

"Man, that girl loves you, ya'll belong together, L.C advised.

"Yeah, maybe one day." Walking back to the truck that he and L.C came in. Well, I got one more call to make." Soulja began dialing the number ."Hey, Detective Wilson."

"Parelli? How the fuck did you get my number?'

"That don't matter, look, I was calling to congratulate you on your medal the feds gave you for stopping the bad guy."

"Yeah, well they'll probably make me captain when I bring yo punk ass in. "The disgruntled detective answered.

"I kind of doubt it. Look, how long have we been playing this game and you haven't won?'

"I got your card Parelli. You fucking believe that shit." Getting out his car in front of his home.

"You have a good night detective." Soulja told him and then hung up. I hate that fucking guy, thought Detective Wilson, walking to his front door.

(Goodnight)

Detective Wilson was returning home from having dinner with some guys from the force, because today he had received a medal for stopping that psycho on that motorcycle who had killed one federal officer and wounded two others. Federal authorities said detective Wilsons quick thinking have saved more lives by stopping the pursuit of Tye when he did. He was still upset he didn't get to put Ronnie Parelli away, but he's still hopeful and Ronnie still out there some where thought Detective Wilson as he put his badge and gun on the night stand by his bed and went to the kitchen to get some water. He turned on the light and the first thing he pays attention to are these fucking safety glasses.

"Soulja told me to tell you, game over.